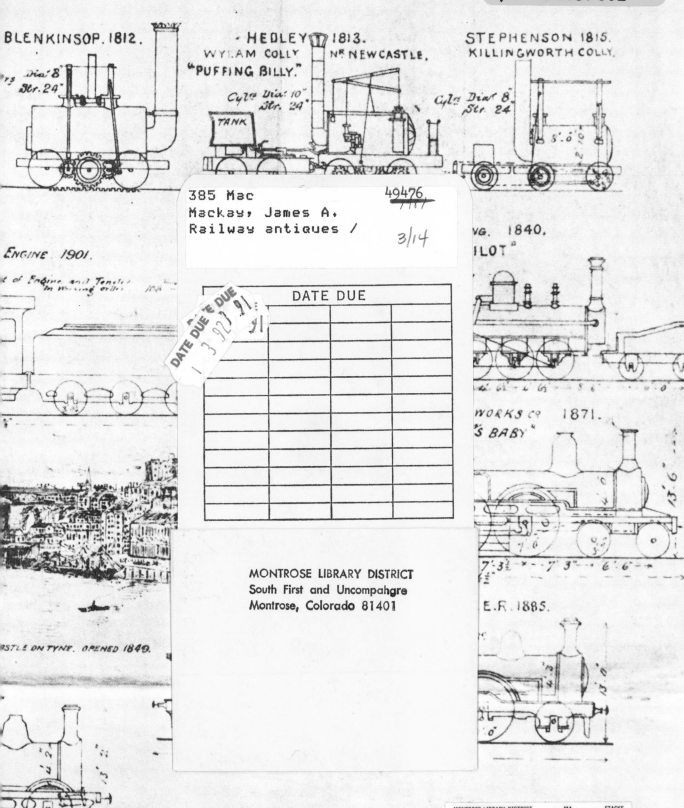

ANTIQUES

JAMES MACKAY

Mayflower/Ward Lock

THE FIRST-CLASS PASSENGER.

© James Mackay 1978

ISBN 0 7063 5526 1

First published in Great Britain 1978 by Ward Lock Limited, London, a member of the Pentos Group. Published in association with Mayflower Books Inc.

Printed in Great Britain

Above One of the plates from the Comic Bradshaw which parodied the famous timetable and lampooned the seasoned first-class passenger of the mid-19th century

Page 1 Seal of the Harrow and Stanmore Railway Company; English, mid-19th century

Page 2 Interior of York Station, England, *c*. 1880

Jacket front

Top (left) Detail from a Southern Railway poster; *(right)* a selection of American railway tickets

Centre Octagonal railway clock from York, England

Bottom (left) A selection of British railway crockery; *(right)* British railway and Trade Union badges and medals

Jacket back

American railway poster, advertising the grand opening of the Union Pacific Platte Valley route, 1869

Jacket flap

Lartigue's monorail on the Listowel–Ballybunnion line, Ireland, 1882. It continued running until 1924.

Contents

Introduction

Unlike most people I cannot recall when I saw my first locomotive, for the simple reason that I spent much of my early childhood in a Scottish mining village whose existence and even its very name were a constant reminder of the coal-burning locomotives in the Age of Steam. The site of the village was a wilderness until 1848, when one of the myriad Acts of Parliament passed that year at the height of the great railway mania authorized a branch line from the Caledonian Railway to the newly discovered Lesmahagow coalfields. The nucleus of the village that developed at the end of that line consisted of miners' rows and railway cottages.

In 1890 my grandfather left the Island of Skye to look for work in the Scottish Lowlands and eventually found employment with the Caledonian Railway as a signalman. When he tried to organize a union of railway workers, he was dismissed and lost his railway cottage into the bargain. By now married, with several children, he took a smallholding on the edge of the village. The extension of the railroad to the colliery ran along the boundary of his croft, and a narrow-gauge mineral line actually traversed his land. The 'hutches' of the mineral line were drawn by ponies, as in the days before the Iron Horse, but the colliery wagons on the branch line were drawn by a motley assortment of steam locomotives. Though the Caledonian Railway had long since been swallowed up by the London, Midland and Scottish in the regrouping of 1921–3, the monogram of the old 'Caley' was still on the station lamps, the trespass signs on the permanent way, and the horological museum piece that graced the wall of the diminutive waiting-room as I remember it during World War II.

During the war the four great railway companies of Britain had been run in the national interest, and afterwards the Labour Government decided that the railway system should be nationalized and transformed into a single organization known as British Railways, and latterly more simply as British Rail. But even the dramatic events of nationalization in 1948, when the LMS gave way in turn to the Scottish Region of British Rail, made little impact on this backwater. In a derelict carriage, lying in a siding rank with weeds, I found a car card bearing a map of the Caledonian Railway, replete with vignettes of its more imposing hotels and stations. This was my

Opposite Framed glass picture of a railway scene; American, mid-19th century

Locomotive *Firefly* hauling a train of the United States Military Railroad, photographed by Matthew Brady during the American Civil War

London, Brighton and South Coast Railway's *Poplar, c.* 1910. Note the oval number plate 70 on the cabside.

first railway antique but, sad to say, it fell victim to spring-cleaning – as, indeed, did other bulkier *objets trouvés* at various times. Perhaps this was a blessing in disguise, for I realized early on that there was little sense in a haphazard accumulation of lamps, telegraph instruments and locomotive name plates which would rapidly have become unmanageable. I decided instead to concentrate on the more compact and convenient ephemera of the railways – the tickets, luggage labels, parcel labels, stationery and stamps.

Nationalization of industry did not turn out to be quite the panacea expected for either the coalmines or the railway in my little village. Instead, nationalization meant the closure of uneconomic pits, and though the branch line won a brief respite, catering for the commuters who managed to find work in Glasgow some thirty miles away, it was one of the first to be closed in that spirit of retrenchment which swept over British Rail in the 50s and 60s, and has since been a feature of the railway systems of the United States and most other Western countries. Today the little village station is no more, unlike the buildings in more fashionable areas which have found a new lease of life as conversions into public bars or private houses. What became of the old oil lamps, the wooden name boards, the enamel signs and the antiquated fittings? I hope that they have found good homes in one of the railway museums or perhaps in the private collections that have proliferated in recent years.

The usual definition of an antique as something more than a hundred years old has been extended in practice to include anything dating before about 1930. With the railways, however, it is possible

Above Photograph by A. J. Russell, *c.* 1868, of the way stop at Little Laramie River, Wyoming. Locomotive No. 23 appears to have been polished specially for this photograph. Note the antlers on the headlight!

Left Cirencester station, England in the 1920s. Note the standard pattern station lamp and also the welter of enamelled advertising signs, which were a characteristic feature of many rural railway stations before World War II

Left French railway postcard of 1900 showing a countryside station scene

Contréxeville. - Arrivée du " Train des Eaux".

to shorten the date-line even further. In Britain, for example, the Transport Act of 1962 was a portent of sweeping changes, developed in Dr Richard Beeching's *Reshaping of British Railways* which was published the following year. In 1964–5 thousands of miles of track were scrapped, entire lines were closed and countless stations disappeared. This Draconian measure coincided with the completion of a modernization programme instituted in 1955 and the withdrawal of the last steam train in 1966 and the Corporate Identity Programme, launched in 1965, which transformed the appearance not only of the locomotives and the rolling-stock but even the uniforms of the railway personnel, the crockery and cutlery, the notepaper, tickets, labels and most trivial items of ephemera.

These dramatic changes were paralleled all over the world. The United States of America with its enormous oil resources was the first country to switch from steam to diesel locomotives in the 30s. Many European countries whose railroad systems were severely disrupted, if not devastated, by World War II had a head start in the race for modernization. Significantly the most impressive array of modern locomotives and rolling-stock ever assembled, as a portent of things to come, was displayed at the Brussels World Fair of 1958. The emphasis today is laid on long-distance lines, from the relatively modest inter-city routes of Britain to the great transcontinental lines of America, Asia and now Africa. The ultra-modern, streamlined, electronically controlled locomotives which cruise at speeds in excess of 100 mph are a far cry from the puffing, hissing, clanking monsters of the Steam Age. In no other field of human endeavour has such a transformation been wrought in so short a time.

Nothing has become the old railways of the world so much as their passing. Paradoxically, as the railways declined in face of competition from airlines and motorways, were nationalized, cut back and modernized, nostalgia for the not-so-good old days of steam has grown in momentum, stimulated by the railway companies themselves who now regard collectors as a lucrative outlet for what might otherwise be unsaleable scrap. A passion for old railroads has now become dignified under the name of industrial archaeology, and the rise and fall of the railways over the past century and a half is the object of serious study by social and economic historians.

The most significant phenomenon of recent years, however, has been the growth of preservation societies which have been formed to revive some of the branch lines of yesteryear and even some lines which became defunct during much earlier periods of retrenchment. This idea seems to have developed out of the success of the Talyllyn Railway, a narrow-gauge line in North Wales which had escaped the fate of larger and more important lines by not having been worth nationalizing in the first place. The success of this modest line, depending largely on the unbounded enthusiasm and hard work of a band of volunteers, encouraged the formation of a number of other

Evening Star – the last major steam locomotive built for British Railways, 1960, and now preserved at the National Railway Museum, York

societies in England and Wales, and more recently in Scotland, which have restored the permanent way and operate scheduled services by steam locomotives. Undoubtedly these little railways began as a tourist attraction, aiming at preserving something of the country's heritage, but in more recent years there has been a significant trend towards the establishment of short commuter lines by private enterprise as a purely commercial undertaking in areas which British Rail has long since abandoned. We are now going through a second railway mania, far less dramatic than that of the 1840s, admittedly; but there is some irony in the fact that in this era of the Advanced Passenger Train the mileage under steam is growing steadily from year to year.

This pattern is being repeated in every other country whose rail system has undergone the same policies of retrenchment and modernization. The restoration of historic narrow-gauge lines is a feature of several American railroad museums, such as the five-mile line through the Cape Cod area around Edaville or the East Broad Top Railroad which once linked Mount Union and the coalmines of central Pennsylvania. British Rail has cashed in on the popularity of these little railways and runs one of its own through the picturesque Vale of Rheidol, while the Kingston Flyer, operated by New Zealand Railways, is now one of the major tourist attractions of the South Island.

During their heyday the railways had a tremendous impact on every aspect of life. They have been immortalized in painting and sculpture and lent inspiration to every field of the applied and decorative arts. The collector of railway antiques is faced with an enormous and exceedingly diverse range of material, both directly produced for and by the railroads themselves and indirectly connected with them – often in the shape of advertising and promotional material. Commemorative wares and items indirectly associated with the railways have long been sought after and are highly elusive nowadays; but the more mundane objects used by the railways are often reasonably plentiful even now owing to obsolescence.

Interest in the artefacts of the old railroads as a serious branch of industrial archaeology first developed in the United States before the war and received tremendous impetus in the late 40s and 50s with the closure of many of the smaller lines. Railroadiana became a regular feature of many of the small town and country auctions held from coast to coast. Bearing in mind that in a period of a century and a quarter there were literally hundreds of railroad companies operating into every part of the North American sub-continent, the scope of collectables is truly enormous. Admittedly, much of this material was dispersed in the late nineteenth century before collector interest was really awakened, but a tremendous amount of railroad material has survived. In the period immediately after World War II many companies sold off surplus material and scrap to collectors, and this is a practice which has since been emulated in other countries, notably Britain. Many of the regional headquarters of British Rail operate collectors' shops and scrap-yards where many of the smaller objects can be purchased quite cheaply. There are now several specialist dealers in railwayana in most Western countries, and many antique shops have railroad items through their hands from time to time. The American custom of specialist auctions of railroad material has now spread to Britain, France, Germany and Italy. Railway material, at one time the closed preserve of the dedicated few, is now of general interest to virtually everyone who collects bygones and therefore may often be found in flea-markets and collectors' fairs.

A major advantage of collecting rail relics is that this is a hobby which can still be tailored to one's financial limits. Few people nowadays would want to collect nothing but the name plates of famous expresses, even if they could afford to do so, but happily there are innumerable categories of antique which can still be collected on a fairly modest budget. This is a relatively new area of collecting where even the beginner may be lucky enough to find interesting and unusual items and make an original contribution to our knowledge of the subject. There is a growing number of museums and societies dedicated to our railway heritage and a wealth of literature from general histories to specialized aspects of individual lines, as well as numerous periodicals which assist the collector to a better understanding of the objects in his chosen field.

While the railway magazines and societies cater for enthusiasts in general and are not designed exclusively for the collector, they offer the best method of acquiring new material or disposing of surplus or unwanted articles through small advertisements and exchange clubs. Membership of such societies enables one to keep abreast of the latest developments and market trends as well as meeting like-minded individuals.

What one collects will be determined largely by the amount of space – and money – available, but it would be wise at the outset to try and form some definite plan. One may concentrate on uniforms,

Below View of Dursley railway station, England, *c.* 1925

Dacre station in the 1920s – a typical example of English railway architecture of the early 20th century, with substantial stone buildings. Many of them have survived the closure of the country lines and have been converted for private use – and even private museums run by some rail enthusiasts.

badges, buttons and insignia, or crested china and cutlery of the railway companies, or posters, pamphlets and brochures, or tickets and labels. Model locomotives and even toy trains are other fields which have a large following, while some collectors specialize in signalling equipment and telegraph instruments. Another approach is to concentrate on the material pertaining to a particular country or even a single company and collect anything and everything across the entire spectrum of railwayana. The restoration, cleaning, care and maintenance of railway relics are largely matters of common sense, but specific problems are discussed where relevant throughout this book.

DACRE

TREVITHICKS,
PORTABLE STEAM ENGINE.

Catch me who can.

Mechanical Power Subduing
Animal Speed.

1 The scope of railway antiques

The railway or railroad as we understand the term is of much greater antiquity than is generally realized. The steam-engine and the use of rails were both employed separately long before George Stephenson brought them together. Trackways of granite setts were used since Roman times to enable horse-drawn vehicles to run more swiftly and smoothly, and by the late Middle Ages wooden rails were used in the iron, coal and silver mines of northern Europe, particularly in Germany, Bohemia and Alsace. There are many woodcuts and engravings dating from the fifteenth century which show wagons hauled by ropes and horses or propelled by men, transporting ore and coal from these mines. Mineral railways and tramways with quite sophisticated layouts were in operation in Britain in the eighteenth century, transporting coal and iron ore from the mines to the canals and seaports.

Many scientists had studied the power of boiling water, from Archimedes and Hero of Alexandria to Leonardo da Vinci and Johannes Branca, but James Watt of Greenock was the first to devise a practical steam-engine complete with cylinder and piston. Stationary engines, operating on the principles discovered by Watt, were used in the collieries of the late eighteenth century to pump out water and haul wagons drawn by cable. In 1769 a French artillery officer, Nicolas Cugnot, invented a steam-carriage which crashed into a wall during its demonstration run in Paris. Patrick Millar operated an experimental steamboat on Dalswinton Loch, Dumfriesshire, in 1787, but a quarter of a century elapsed before the problems of steam applied to shipping were overcome by William Symington's *Charlotte Dundas* which plied on the Forth and Clyde Canal in 1802. Robert Fulton fitted steam-engines by Boulton and Watt of Birmingham into a paddle-steamer in 1807 and ran it on the Hudson river.

It seemed as though steam-engines were better suited to boats than land vehicles. Both Oliver Evans in America and Richard Trevithick in England experimented with steam-carriages at the beginning of the nineteenth century, and to the latter goes the honour of constructing the first railway locomotive in 1804.

Almost as complex in their evolution as the engines themselves were the rails. Rails of oak construction were introduced in England

Opposite Broadsheet advertising Trevithick's *Catch me who can*, 1808

in 1676 and were connected by sills secured with oak trenails. A later development was the sleeper, tie or cross-piece covered with earth to protect the horses' hooves. These comparatively elaborate railroads, laid by permission of local landowners, were known as way-leaves. In the early eighteenth century it became customary to attach bars of wrought iron to the tops of the wooden rails to protect them against wear, and this system survived in many places for more than a hundred years. Oddly enough this compound of wood and iron was used on the earliest American railroads. As the ends of the bars became loose and turned upwards they were known as 'snakes-heads' and occasionally they ripped through the floors of the primitive carriages and injured passengers.

Solid rails of cast iron with flanges, or ledged on their inner side to keep the wheel on the track, were first produced by the Coal-brookdale Iron Company of Shropshire in 1767. These flanges were known as trammels because they 'trammelled' or confined the wheel to the rail. Lines bearing these flanged rails therefore came to be called trammel-roads, later abbreviated to tramroads or tramways. A variant of this was the flanged wheel invented by Jessop of Loughborough in 1789, and this ran on an edged rail. Jessop also invented the system of laying rails on iron chairs which were bolted to the sleepers. In 1820 came Birkenshaw's 'fish-belly' rail and this remained standard for a decade, but when steam locomotives were actually put into service it was found to be unsatisfactory, so then the more efficient flat-bottomed rail was devised.

All the later forms of steel rail derived from the flat-bottomed or flat-foot of 1830, and examples of the double-headed and bull-headed rails, developed in the 1840s, together with the distinctive iron chairs and even the bolts and spikes and fish-plates required to secure them belong to the archaeology of the railway. Long neglected and overshadowed by the more showy forms of rail relic, they are now receiving the serious attention of the industrial archaeologist who retrieves them from disused collieries and long-defunct lines, using metal detectors and all the other scientific aids now available.

In July 1803 the Surrey Iron Railway from Wandsworth (then a London suburb) to Croydon in Surrey was opened to the public. This, the world's first commuter train, was hauled by horses. Horse-drawn trams and streetcars eventually became a familiar sight in many towns and cities on both sides of the Atlantic and were only gradually superseded, from the late nineteenth century onwards, by electrically operated cars. At one time, however, it seemed as though freight and passenger trains would also be drawn by horses. The Budweis-Linz railway in Bohemia (now part of Czechoslovakia) was opened in 1832 with horse-drawn wagons for freight and passengers and was not converted to steam locomotives until 1857.

A few months after the Surrey Iron Railway was inaugurated, Richard Trevithick made history by operating a more advanced

Trevithick demonstrating *Catch me who can* in Euston Square, London, from a print by Rowlandson, 1809

version of his steam locomotive on a mineral way-leave at Merthyr Tydfil in South Wales. Thereafter his locomotive regularly pulled wagons loaded with 10 tons of iron ore at a speed of 8 mph. In 1808 he demonstrated his passenger locomotive *Catch me who can* on a special track near Gower Street in London, charging a shilling a ride, but the rails were unequal to the weight imposed on them and the locomotive was swiftly derailed.

For several years the steam-carriage was little more than a curiosity. It was a demonstration by Trevithick in Newcastle that is said to have inspired George Stephenson to take up the challenge. He improved on the designs of Trevithick and others and built his own 'travelling machine' which made its debut at Killingworth on 25 July 1814. With that flair for showmanship which was to prove invaluable in later years he named his locomotive *Blücher* after Wellington's Prussian ally at the recent Battle of Waterloo. *Blücher* hauled eight wagons with a load of 30 tons at 10 mph. The age of speed was just around the corner.

In the ensuing decade Stephenson and his son Robert built more than fifty locomotives, most of which were destined to haul coal trucks along the mineral lines of the north of England. In 1823 they established a factory in Newcastle – the world's first custom-built locomotive workshop – and a year later won the contract to build a railroad from the colliery town of Darlington in County Durham to the seaport of Stockton on the Tees estuary, a distance of twelve miles. The earlier mineral railways often varied considerably in gauge with tracks up to 7 ft in width, but now Stephenson laid down the gauge which was to become standard not only in Britain but throughout much of the world. His gauge of 4 ft 8½ in was the same as that of the mail coaches then in use and was in turn based on the supposed gauge of the Roman chariots!

Hitherto the mineral railroads were concerned with the carriage of freight, but Stephenson envisaged the immense possibilities of passenger traffic as well and accordingly designed carriages on the same lines as contemporary stage-coaches, complete with coachman's box and luggage racks on the roof. The Stockton and Darlington Railway was inaugurated on 27 June 1825, and the handbills advertising the event are among the most highly prized of railway antiques today. On that epoch-making occasion George Stephenson himself drove the prosaically named *Locomotion No. 1* which pulled thirty-four wagons and coaches carrying the railway workmen and their families, interested spectators, members of the railway company, the local landowners and nobility – some 600 passengers in all.

From the collector's viewpoint the opening of the Stockton and Darlington Railway has yielded a wealth of memorabilia. The occasion was recorded in sundry broadsheets and popular prints, in commemorative medals, plaques and pottery. The more ephemeral items included the ornate tickets for the workmen's dinner and the elegant banquet held in Darlington Town Hall. Ancillary items of great interest and value include the share certificates when the company was launched in 1821, various pamphlets published for and against the railway at the planning stage and copies of the Acts of Parliament that sanctioned it. Anniversaries of the event, the jubilee in 1875, the centenary in 1925 and the sesquicentennial in 1975, have all added their quota of collectables. Few other railway engineers excited public interest as much as George Stephenson, and a sizeable collection could be made of the bronze and plaster statuettes, busts and profile bas-reliefs, the rack-plates, mugs and

Opposite Driving cab of a 'push and pull' locomotive of the Great Eastern Railway. Note the anti-spitting notice.

Right Obverse and reverse of the silver medal commemorating the 150th anniversary of the world's first public railway – the Stockton and Darlington, England, 1825

tankards, the scarves and kerchiefs and popular prints which portrayed him and depicted one or other of his pioneer locomotives.

Actual items of railwayana associated with the early lines are, not surprisingly, of the greatest rarity. Many of the prototype locomotives, or contemporary models of them, have survived, but the majority of them are now preserved in museums. The same is true of the early locomotives of the United States whose premier line, the Baltimore and Ohio Railroad of 1829, is enshrined in the Transportation Museum in Baltimore, though the earliest actual locomotive there is the *Grasshopper* built in 1832.

Early accessories and equipment often remained in use long after the original line was amalgamated with others, and when they became unserviceable they were destroyed. Consequently many of the more mundane articles, particularly the uniforms of railway personnel up to about 1890, are relatively scarce. The same is true of implements and utensils which eventually wore out and were thrown on the scrap-heap. These objects had no intrinsic, aesthetic or curiosity value, and in the days before collectors and preservationists no one consciously laid them aside for posterity. Even objects of more recent vintage have often survived by pure chance. Often it is the smaller articles, such as office date-stamps, seals and guards' whistles, which have been inadvertently preserved at the back of a drawer until unearthed many years after they were rendered obsolete.

The scope of railway antiques also varies considerably from one country to another. Many of the objects discussed in this book depend for their range and scope on the variety of the companies and groupings that used them. A multiplicity of small companies and lines in a country will result not only in a complete lack of standardization in the design, size and composition of such items as oilcans, signal padlocks, baggage checks and tools but also in an infinite variety of motifs in the monograms and crests found on carriage panels, tableware and even tickets. This is true of the American railroads up to the present day and applied also, to a lesser extent, to the British companies of the pre-grouping era. The Act of 1921 forced the railways of Britain into four large groups, and the identities of the constituent companies and their subsidiaries then disappeared. For this reason the relics of the pre-grouping era are much sought after by collectors specializing in a particular line or locality.

At the other extreme are those countries which had a state-controlled railway network from the beginning. The Belgian railways from their inception in 1834 were state-owned. In Germany the multitude of small lines, many of them owned by individual states, were gradually brought under Prussian control, though even after 1875 the states of Bavaria and Württemberg continued to exercise a certain amount of autonomy over their railways. Seven of the major companies in France amalgamated in 1850, and state intervention in

Polished brass handbell used by the North-Eastern Railway; British, *c.* 1890

1878 prevented a number of other companies from going into liquidation. Since then the Société Nationale de Chemins de Fer Français (SNCF) has gradually absorbed many private lines, though a few continue to exist independently to this day. The scope for collectors of relics associated with the railways of Belgium, Germany and France thus varies considerably, and again emphasis is laid on the period of true antiques, a century ago, for the greatest diversity.

Most of the succeeding chapters in this book deal with the equipment, accessories, furniture and other objects produced for or by the railways themselves. What they may lack in their often humdrum appearance is compensated by the romantic attachment of these objects with historic trains and companies. The actual whip-poorwill whistle blown by Casey Jones[1] would be infinitely preferable to the rarest piece of railway pottery or a Stevengraph of the

[1] Even the Casey Jones Museum in Jackson, Tennessee, has only a replica.

WOVEN IN PURE SILK BY THOMAS STEVENS, STEVENGRAPH WORKS, COVENTRY.

The Mersey Tunnel Railway.

Stevengraph of the Mersey Tunnel, England, 1886

Rocket. Fortunately there are few instances like this where association with a famous railroad engineer is likely to enhance the value of a utilitarian object to any real extent.

Many of the objects of railwayana were produced by the railway companies to advertise themselves to the public and ranged from picture postcards, posters and travel brochures to giveaways like paperweights, trays, coasters and beer mats, pens and pencils and even children's board games illustrating scenic routes and landmarks on their lines. Much of this material was ephemeral and is now decidedly scarce. Again, promotional material of this type was most plentiful in the United States and Canada where the competition between many different companies was keen and all the weapons of publicity and advertising were utilized to the full.

Then there are all the collectables which are only indirectly connected with the railways. Quite apart from the commemorative wares – a field that is growing steadily as more and more of the world's railroads celebrate centenaries and sesquicentennials – there are numerous souvenirs and decorative articles which have a rail motif. The most desirable of these belong to the period up to about 1860 when the railway was still a novelty and had a tremendous impact on commerce and industry and even the way people lived. It is difficult in this modern age to appreciate how the coming of the railroad revolutionized every aspect of life in the mid-nineteenth century. Communications were accelerated beyond belief, natural resources, hitherto untapped, were suddenly brought into use, whole

26

towns and villages sprang up along the railroad tracks, large areas of unexplored territory were opened up, and major industries from heavy engineering to tourism were created virtually overnight. The Iron Horse, the wonder of the age, embellished countless objects – from watchcases to chairbacks, from bandboxes to beer bottles. At a somewhat later date the distinctive shape of locomotives lent itself to all manner of containers – from glass candy jars to biscuit tins, from pencil-sharpeners to pepper-pots. There was seemingly no end to the novelties which could be fashioned in the image of the steam-engine and its carriages.

Most of the railway antiques mentioned in this book relate to the steam locomotive, but it would be foolish to ignore the collectables associated with other forms of locomotion. Indeed, experiments with other methods of traction or propulsion have a surprisingly long history. As early as 1842 Robert Davidson ran a 5-ton electric locomotive on the Edinburgh and Glasgow Railway, but it was hardly practical as its maximum speed was a mere 4 mph. Werner von Siemens constructed an electric motor in 1879, and only four years later Magnus Volk opened his electric railway at Brighton; the collectables in this instance range from the illustrated pamphlet sold for a penny at the inauguration in August 1883 down to the tickets and postcards of more modern times. Electric streetcars, elevated

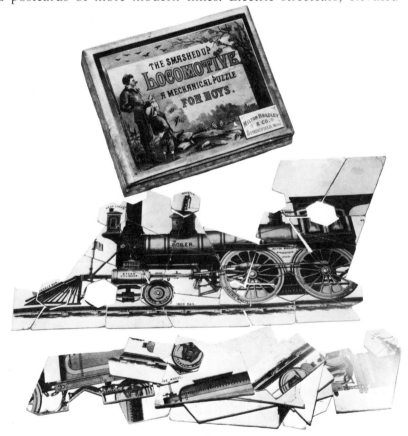

The Smashed up Locomotive: a mechanical puzzle for boys, a dissected puzzle produced by the Milton Bradley Company of Springfield, Mass., in 1868

Leaflet advertising the exhibition marking the Diamond Jubilee of the Great Northern Railway, Minneapolis, 1924

railways and underground railways became widespread at the turn of the century, and extensive railway networks using electricity were developed in countries with an abundant supply of hydro-electric power after World War I, notably Switzerland, Bavaria and Norway.

Rudolf Diesel invented the engine that still bears his name in 1897. The early diesel locomotives were beset with many problems and were consequently subject to numerous modifications. It was not until the development of the diesel-electric motor in the 1930s that transmission problems were finally solved. Many of the early diesels were produced in the United States and other countries which had a ready supply of crude oil. In the period between the two World Wars there were experiments with internal combustion engines in railcars intended for service on short feeder lines and in remote rural areas and experiments with streamlined, lightweight railcars, such as Franz Kruckenberg's propeller-driven 'Zeppelin on Rails'. Fritz von Opel, the famous automobile engineer, even invented a rocket-propelled railcar which attained a speed in excess of 250 mph before it exploded.

The monorail, which even now has scarcely passed beyond the experimental stage, has an amazing antiquity dating back to 1821 when Henry Robinson Palmer demonstrated a horse-drawn vehicle running on a single rail – though he cheated by using tiny side wheels as stabilizers. The first real monorail was that invented by an Irishman, Louis Brennan, using gyroscopes to maintain equilibrium. Though he successfully demonstrated his monorail in 1907, the general lack of faith in gyroscopes deterred potential backers. The Spanish inventor Lartigue constructed a form of monorail which ran successfully between Listowel and Ballybunion in Ireland as long ago as 1882 – yet seventy years elapsed before this idea was perfected and given practical expression by the *Alwegbahn* (an acronym from the initials of its promoter Axel Leonard Wenner-Gren) which was inaugurated near Cologne in 1952. A variation of this is the *Schwebebahn,* or suspension railway, in which the train is suspended from a single rail. Such railways have been running for many years in Germany where they serve short-haul commuter traffic. A similar device was the Rail-plane invented by a Glasgow industrialist, George Bennie, in 1930. The Rail-plane, like a silver torpedo, hung from its test-track and was an impressive landmark on the outskirts of Glasgow for many years. Now, alas, it has disappeared and is remembered only by a handful of souvenirs, from the promotional literature of the company to the prewar postcards and cigarette cards which depicted it. In America the monorail was a striking feature of the Century 21 Exposition in Seattle and is also one of the major attractions of Disneyland. The tickets and other ephemera produced in this connection may be of minor interest at this moment – but they will rank among the railway antiques of the future.

Other aspects of the railways which are now beginning to attract serious attention overlap with hobbyists in other fields. Railway philately (discussed in Chapter 6) is the most prominent of these and has had its devotees as long as any other branch of railwayana, but among the more recent areas of interest are the security and military aspects. Security guards and railway police have had distinctive insignia, uniforms, firearms, handcuffs and truncheons for over a century. Military railways often form a distinctive corps, especially in European armies, or an important branch of the Engineers, as in Britain and the United States. The strategic importance of railroads was forcibly demonstrated in the American Civil War when entire armies and their artillery were moved rapidly by rail, and ever since the railways have played a major role in most wars. The Canadian Forestry Corps built light railways in the Scottish Highlands in World War I, and personnel of the American Engineer Corps built and repaired track and bridges in every theatre of operations in World War II. The Allied prisoners who worked and died on the infamous Siamese Railway are recalled by grim mementoes of the 1940s.

In this brief survey of railway antiques it should not be overlooked that at various times the railways have diversified into other modes of transport. These range from station carts drawn by ponies to horse-charabancs and motor buses connecting rail routes, and they have yielded a fine crop of memorabilia from horse brasses to tickets and timetables. But there are also the train ferries from paddle-steamers to modern hovercraft and even such curiosities as the Railway Air Service which operated in Britain in the 30s and used distinctive stamps and stationery. Truly there are few aspects of life that have not been touched by the railways at some time or another, and therein lies much of the appeal of railway antiques to so many collectors all over the world.

Wooden cylinder with attached paper roll showing a coloured aquatint of the journey. This ingenious device produced by an enterprising English publisher, c. 1845, was an early attempt to divert the passenger's attention from the tedium of the journey and indicate the landmarks *en route*.

2 Parts and accessories

There are very few collectors who would today aspire to owning an actual locomotive, but there are countless bits and pieces associated with trains which are treasured almost as much and present far fewer problems. The severe pruning of uneconomic lines which has taken place in most countries in recent years has brought to light a vast amount of material which has been eagerly snapped up by collectors. The present businesslike approach of the railway companies in the sale of their relics has tended to rob railwayana of some of the excitement when a much less formal arrangement existed – if at all. In the good old days when railway enthusiasts were regarded as harmless eccentrics the companies were often only too glad to give away obsolete equipment or allow collectors to roam like hungry magpies over their scrap-heaps and junkyards. Gone are the days of derelict loco-sheds and overgrown sidings where the cinders and rotting sleepers were paved with gold – in the collector's eyes at least. But the old, unregulated system was bad in many respects. Many priceless items which ought to have been preserved for posterity were lost for ever, and much that did eventually get into the hands of collectors was in poor, neglected condition by the time it was rescued.

Many of the items discussed here are three-dimensional, often bulky or heavy, and may require considerable care and maintenance, not to mention actual restoration. Many of them pose serious problems of housing and display, and the walls of the typical modern house, for example, would not be able to bear the strain if decorated with an assortment of locomotive name plates or cast-iron wayside signs. Nevertheless, the parts and accessories connected with the actual locomotives, carriages and stations are a field that few collectors can resist.

Locomotive parts

The very earliest locomotives were almost naïve in their simplicity, but their constructors quickly learned the hard way that steam-engines had no future if they could not be mastered. A primitive brake on the locomotive was worse than useless if there was no means of braking the carriages and wagons simultaneously – as early

Opposite Pair of brass Lucas 'King of the Road' oil side-lamps, each with red bullseye to the rear and clear glass to the front

Right Cast-brass steam-heater control lever; British, early 20th century

Above Locomotive steam whistle; British, late 19th century

Opposite Interior of a very ornate dining-car from the National Railway Museum, York, England

derailments and disasters soon proved. Similarly, it was not sufficient – as one unfortunate engineer discovered – to try to control the steam escaping from a leaky valve merely by sitting on it. By the time of the Rainhill Trials in October 1829 George Stephenson had ironed out most of the problems revealed by *Locomotion No. 1* and incorporated many refinements and safety features in his *Rocket,* which won the contest and the contract for the Liverpool and Manchester Railway and established the ascendancy of the Iron Horse over the four-footed variety.

Stylistically there were many developments in the years to come, but the fundamental principles of the steam locomotive remained almost unchanged from 1830 onwards. Among the improvements which Stephenson introduced at that time were the brass boiler tubes which enabled the hot gases to heat the water much more rapidly and the elaborate system of cocks and gauges which kept the unruly monster under control. Funnels, domes and safety valves, taps, levers and cocks were beautifully constructed in copper or brass which the driver and his fireman kept meticulously polished. Considering the primitive tools available at the time, the precision of these early valves and gauges is quite remarkable. When locomotives were sent to the breakers' yards, the non-ferrous metal parts were salvaged for their scrap value, but quite a few seem to have been purloined as mementoes. The more desirable examples are those which bear an inscription identifying the instrument maker, the locomotive builder or the railroad company, and the incorporation of dates and serial numbers enhances their value. The steam whistles, horns and bells fitted to the locomotive cab were also made of brightly burnished brass and are among the most attractive items. They come in all shapes and sizes and include examples

with double or treble tones producing highly distinctive notes. Bells and whistles became standard pieces of equipment within a decade of the establishment of railways and were intended to give warning to cattle and pedestrians of the train's approach.

Engine parts are decidedly scarce since being made of iron or steel they were not usually salvaged separately like the brass levers and cocks. Other brass fittings which have survived, however, include the rims of the funnels, the domed safety-valve covers and the safety rails which were mounted alongside the boiler. Some of these rails had most elaborate knobs and finials with crowns, lions' masks and a variety of other forms of decoration, and these are prized accordingly.

Although the early enginemen took great pride in polishing the brasswork, for reasons of economy and manpower-saving a number of companies at various times have resorted to the coating of brass and copper with paint or enamel in sombre shades of brown and black. Where possible this external coating should be carefully stripped, using one of the many paint solvents now available, and cleaned and polished to its pristine condition. Soot-impregnated grease and grime can be removed by washing in warm, soapy water, and working parts should be lightly oiled. Rust is more of a problem since steel wool and other harsh abrasives should never be used except in the very last resort. There are various patent rust removers on the market today which alleviate the situation, but there is no substitute for patience and elbow grease. There are clear varnishes which protect copper and brass without concealing their beauty, but the true enthusiast usually prefers to polish the metalwork regularly, seeing this as a labour of love rather than an irksome chore.

The earliest trains ran during the daylight hours only but by 1840 they were running at night and also in all weathers. Lighting thus became a necessity for a variety of reasons. Most important was the headlight attached to the front of the locomotive on the buffer bar or smoke-box door with a powerful beam to light up the permanent way for the engine-driver. The early lamps were oil-burning and may be found in a vast range of sizes and types, themselves illustrating the development of the oil-lamp in the nineteenth century. From the technical standpoint there are slip burners, Duplex burners, Argand, Carcel and Moderator lamps, incandescent lamps like the Kronos or the Candesco, the ubiquitous Aladdin and the German Practicus. They were fitted with patent draught excluders, elaborate reflectors and magnifiers and were housed in copper-sheathed, japanned or enamelled containers of enormous variety in design. Though electric and battery lamps began to replace them by the end of the last century, many of them remained in service in the remoter parts of the world until fairly recently. Brass filler caps, securing chains and handles added to the attractive appearance of these old lamps. By a combination of headlight and buffer lamps the type and composition

Above Locomotive steam whistle; British, late 19th century

Opposite Variety of crockery, from egg-cup to serving-dish, used by British railway companies in the late 19th century

Lancaster's patent 'Rubralux' lamp with red and green glasses; British

of a train could be identified, and many of the old companies devised quite complex head codes.

Marker lamps or tail-lights with three-aspect bullseye lenses were fitted at the rear of passenger and freight trains. Lighting within the cab was provided by hanging lamps, and there was also a variety of handlamps which were only gradually superseded by carbide lamps and then battery torches in the early years of this century. Many of the old railway companies provided their employees with handlamps designed for each specific task. The American railroads in particular raised lampmanship to the status of a fine art with distinctive lights for the engineer, fireman and conductor and particularly impressive ones for the railroad car inspector.

Undoubtedly the most distinctive and highly prized parts of the actual locomotive were the various name and number plates. These aids to the identity of individual locomotives were probably the first relics to be systematically saved when engines were consigned to the scrap-yard. At first salvaged out of sentiment, they soon became the prime target of the railway collector. The practice of identifying locomotives in this way, however, has varied from country to country and even from company to company. Many American locomotives did not have separate plates but had the numbers painted in large figures on the sides of the tender. Others went to the other extreme and had highly decorative plaques affixed to the smoke-box door. This practice continued into the era of the diesel and electric locos in the years immediately before World War II. In

European countries number plates were to be found in all manner of places: on the cabside, the smoke-box and even (in Russia) attached to the side of the funnel. In Britain loco number plates were mounted on the cabsides or the smoke-box door, depending on the company. The position of the number plate governed the size – funnel, smoke-box door and cabside plates being in ascending order of size. Most of these plates were fairly prosaic in appearance – usually rectangular, occasionally with chamfered corners and sometimes elliptical. The majority are of painted or enamelled iron with raised numerals either in brass or painted in a contrasting colour.

Other plates, very much smaller in size, were usually cast in brass and bear combinations of numbers and letters to indicate the shed code of the motive power department to which the locomotive was allocated. These shed plates in the form of small elliptical plaques were fitted as a rule to the smoke-box door. Similar items, but of greater general interest, are the works plates which usually give the maker's name and address, the date of manufacture and the works' serial number. The scope in works plates is enormous, bearing in mind the large number of locomotive builders that have existed at one time or another – thirty-eight in Scotland alone and well over a hundred in the United States. The value of these plates depends on

Far left Bullseye handlamp used on American railroads in the late 19th century

Left Brass handlamp used by the station-master at Wolferton, England, *c.* 1900

Engraved brass door plate from the Darlington North Road locomotive works; British, 1863

An interesting builder's plate for the North-Eastern Railway, dated 1922 – the year in which the company was absorbed into the London and North-Eastern Railway

the company concerned, the smaller, less successful and more obscure builder being obviously much rarer than the big companies. Plates with early dates and those from companies which have long since disappeared are the most desirable. More modern plates are of less interest, being die-struck from light brass and aluminium alloy sheet. They lack the substance and the deeply incised lettering of the older examples.

While every locomotive had a number, the practice of bestowing names on them varied from company to company. Some lines named everything on wheels from the humblest tank engine to the main-line expresses – often with ludicrous results. Most railway companies, however, reserved names for their more important locomotives. When collectors were not so thick on the ground, they could afford to be choosy about name plates, showing a preference for those which had come from the more famous locomotives, followed by such aesthetic criteria as the style and ornament of the lettering. Before World War I, for example, the British companies produced a very wide range of name plates. Some had the name engraved and embellished with decorative flourishes which have an almost sculptural quality. Others employed raised lettering in brass with the background picked out in a contrasting colour. The size and shape of name plates varied considerably, depending on company practice. Usually plates were attached to the splasher covering the driving-wheels but could be either curved above it or mounted in front of it. Castle-class locomotives had their names split into two with twin plates mounted on adjoining splashers. With the advent of stream-lining and the adoption of a single long splasher to enclose both driving-wheels, name plates tended to become straight and elongated. Clan crests, regimental badges and family coats of arms were among the heraldic devices which were incorporated in name plates where appropriate. This thematic policy was taken to its logical conclusion

by the major British lines of the post-grouping period. Thus locomotives of the 'Merchant Navy' class (Southern Railway) had name
plates embellished with the house flag of the relevant shipping line,
while the Hunt class (London and North-Eastern Railway) had a
running fox above the name plate, and the Battle of Britain class (also
Southern Railway) bore the crest of the Royal Air Force.

Much rarer than the name plates were the headboards which
appeared on the front of the locomotives on titled trains. The
Cambrian bore the red dragon of Wales, while the Cornishman had a
Cornish pisky leaping over a toadstool, but the majority of the British
headboards had no pictorial device. By contrast the American
headboards were lavish affairs, and those on Russian trains had a
large red five-pointed star bearing the profile of Lenin or the
conjoined profiles of Lenin and Stalin during the latter's rule. Such

Above The distinctive Wyvern emblem of the Midland Railway
at the turn of the century

Below Some of the LNER name plates
on display at the National Railway
Museum, York, England

39

headboards were interchangeable and allocated to the major expresses. Relatively few of them have ever come on to the market and most of them are now preserved in museum collections.

The rarest and most colourful of all the headboards are those brought out on very special occasions and used to decorate trains for presidential tours, royal visits, state funerals and the like. Visitors to the National Railway Museum at York can see the special headboards which adorned the royal trains used by Queen Victoria and even the elaborate draped coat of arms which was mounted on the running plate abeam the smoke-box of the Great Western Railway's locomotive *Royal Sovereign* which bore her coffin from Paddington to Windsor in 1901.

At the other extreme are the more functional name plates which were introduced after World War II and fitted to diesel and electric locomotives. The tendency nowadays is for fewer of these engines to be named, though happily this practice shows no sign of dying out.

The tremendous upsurge of interest in rail relics in the past decade or so has created a number of problems for collectors. The price of genuine name plates has rocketed sky-high, and this has encouraged a number of companies, and even British Rail itself, to manufacture excellent replicas. Those which are substantially smaller than the originals or cast in a lightweight aluminium alloy instead of brass will not deceive anyone; but those which in size and material are akin to the genuine article are a potential source of headaches in years to come, despite the claims of the manufacturers that production is strictly controlled. Ironically these name plates and replica works plates which are also produced by British Rail are costly to produce. On these grounds alone the makers claim that such replicas are a good investment and 'antiques of the future', but by destroying the confidence of collectors they may do irreparable damage to this aspect of the railwayana market.

Carriage, wagon and car accessories

The majority of the 600 passengers on the inaugural run of the Stockton and Darlington Railway in 1825 were content to sit on hard wooden benches hastily improvised in open chaldron wagons, normally used for carrying coal and iron ore. Once the novelty of rail transport wore off, the public were bound to demand something better, and the early companies inevitably turned to the coachbuilders who had designed and constructed the stage-coaches. At first, however, only the first-class passengers could travel in reasonable comfort in a passable replica of a stage-coach. Even the second-class passengers had to ride in wagons which had neither roof nor seating, and one shudders to think what sort of accommodation was provided for mere third-class travellers. Competition between the different companies inevitably compelled them to raise their

General view of the Great Eastern Railway dining-car. Note the elaborate mouldings on the ceiling, the advertising cards, discreet by modern standards, and the sumptuous upholstery and monogrammed antimacassars

standards. By the 1850s some form of roof had become more or less obligatory for all classes, though the interior furnishings might leave much to be desired. In 1875 the Midland Railway shook its competitors by abolishing the old third-class carriages and redesignating the second-class as third-class. The other companies rapidly followed suit, and for many years – well into the era of British Rail – the passenger trains of Britain had only first- and third-class carriages. In more recent years this curious anomaly has disappeared, and carriages are now more logically labelled first- and second-class. American trains were nominally of one class, but there were supplements for parlour and dining-cars.

In the days when train journeys were limited to a few miles at most the comfort of passengers was of little importance. Some companies' ideas of passenger comfort were limited to the thoughtful provision of holes in the floors of the wagons, ostensibly to allow rainwater to drain away! As journeys became longer, some provision for the wants of nature had to be made, and by the 1850s some railways had rudimentary toilet facilities rigged up in the baggage car. When the train stopped at a station, there was an undignified rush to the baggage car, and it was not until the introduction of the first corridor trains in 1890 with lavatories incorporated at either end that this problem was eased. Toilet-paper holders, chain-pulls and taps were all decorated with the emblem or cipher of the railway company and have now become eminently collectable.

The first night train ran from Vienna to Berlin via Breslau as long ago as 1847, but no attempt to provide sleeping facilities was made until 1870. Both pillows and rugs could be hired at stations and these, being prominently marked or embroidered with the company's initials, are now much sought after – as well as the distinctive tickets and notices regarding their hire. In many countries night trains provided 'Ladies Only' compartments with distinctive signs which may be found in several languages.

The completion of the Transcontinental Railroad in 1869, linking the Central and Union Pacific lines, brought the era of long-distance rail travel to America, and it was there that the first of the long, single-compartment cars were used, with doors at either end connecting with adjoining cars and also with specialized carriages fitted out as club-cars, smoking-cars and dining-cars. But more than a decade before the American continent was finally spanned by rail, the enormous distances involved in the established routes along the Atlantic seaboard or from New York to Chicago induced the railroad companies to experiment with sleeping-cars. George Mortimer

Illustration from a timetable of the Compagnie Internationale des Wagons-Lits, *c.* 1900

Kitchen of the Great Eastern Railway dining-car, *c.* 1890, complete with coal-fired cooking range

Pullman, a small carpenter and coachbuilder in Albion, N.Y., was commissioned by the Field Brothers of New York to build two prototype sleeping-cars for the Chicago and Alton and the Galena and Chicago Union railroads in 1858. Pullman's answer was to convert two obsolete day cars into crude bunk dormitories with a few drapes providing a bare travesty of privacy between the bunks.

Eye-witness accounts indicate that the Pullman sleeping-cars, the later drawing-room cars and the much-vaunted Palace dining-cars which he pioneered at the end of the Civil War fell woefully short of their advertisements. Pullman's early success was due not to the palatial comfort of his cars (which were shoddy and uncomfortable despite their superficial air of opulence) but to the genius of his advertising copywriters and artists. The posters and leaflets which extolled the merits of 'these palatial Pullman hotel cars' and even renamed the Chicago and Alton as 'the great Palace reclining-chair route' are colourful relics of the first great advertising campaign in rail history. Its success is measured by the fact that Pullman forced his competitors out of business and even beat the redoubtable Andrew Carnegie himself in securing the lucrative contracts for the Trans-continental route.

43

By the turn of the century Pullman was, indeed, a byword for luxury on wheels; but it was stiff competition from the Belgian Nagelmackers and other European entrepreneurs which forced Pullman to raise his standards if he were to succeed in the world markets. The heyday of the great continental expresses, the *trains de luxe,* was the Edwardian era dominated by the Orient Express, Le Train Bleu (which even had a Diaghilev Ballet named in its honour), the Trans-Siberian and America's own Twentieth Century Limited, inaugurated when the new century was only a few months old.

Today, of course, there are still great intercontinental expresses, such as the Trans-Europe, but significantly the most recent developments have been in the Third World of Asia, Africa and Latin America. Few of these long-distance trains measure up to the standards of Pullman and Nagelmackers at their best, except in Australasia where New Zealand's Endeavour, Silver Fern and Southerner expresses present something of the glamour more often associated with air travel and Australia's Indian-Pacific Express, on the 2,400-mile route linking Sydney and Perth, provides comfort and cuisine unparalleled anywhere else in the world. This train, half a mile in length, with its cocktail bar and music room, its individual compartments each equipped with shower and toilet, its lounges and observation car, proves that a luxury service is still possible.

For the most part, however, the great trains are but a shadow of their former grandeur, and cheese-paring functionalism has replaced the splendour and opulence of the early 1900s. Examples of these palaces on wheels are preserved in the various railway museums of Europe and America, and countless fitments and accessories from them have been dispersed to provide a rich field for the collector.

At the upper end of the scale there are the silk-tasselled cords and straps, the richly gilded mirrors, the elegant frosted glass bulbs and fretted metalwork of the table- and wall-lamps, the upholstered footstools and head-rests and the embroidered antimacassars of these *trains de luxe.* At the other end of the scale, however, there are more modest items which are not without considerable interest. There are the stout leather straps, embossed with the company initials or badge, which were once used to raise and lower the window on the doors of compartments, the brass or cast-iron heating regulators, and even the cloth-covered foot-warmers of copper or brass which were used before the advent of heating systems. Particularly desirable are the foot-warmers of fused acetate of soda, solid when cold but liquid when heated. As the acetate changed back to the solid state it gave out heat for a prolonged period.

The railway companies were always conscious of the power of advertising and at a very early date appreciated that rail passengers were the captive audience *par excellence.* Car cards and handbills were a feature of early omnibuses and streetcars, and this practice was extended to many of the inter-urban commuter lines. This form

First-class dining-car of the Great Eastern Railway, showing the crockery, cutlery and table linen in use in the late 19th century

of advertising continues to the present day and is discussed at greater length in Chapter 8. Apart from this ephemera, however, there were more substantial and less blatant forms of advertising which also served to decorate the railway compartment. A few companies had advertising slogans worked into the decorative features on finger panels and door handles, the best known being the slogan 'Live in Metroland' used by the Metropolitan Railway when it ventured forth into wildest Buckinghamshire after World War I and co-operated with the land developers and speculative builders of the 20s to lure London's overspill population out into the Green Belt.

More tasteful and attractive were the carriage panel prints, framed, glazed and mounted on the walls separating the compartments. Artists were commissioned by the rail companies to paint the landmarks and scenic beauties of the various routes, and these were then reproduced as mezzotints, aquatints and latterly chromolithographs. A more direct form of advertisement was the map of the line, sometimes embellished with tiny vignettes of the attractions *en route*, and least subtle of all, the miniature cards which reproduced posters advertising the company, its trains and its hotels. Although reproductions of paintings survived right to the end of this era, photography had a big impact on carriage panel prints from 1900 onwards. Sepia photographs of stations, company hotels and general views of tourist resorts were widely used before and after World War I and survived, anachronistically, on some of the remoter routes even after nationalization in the late 40s, rather pointlessly highlighting the merits of the North British or the West Highland railways.

These panel prints disappeared in the early 50s, the last vestige of this once great art being the purely functional diagrams of the routes covered by the Southern Region which lingered on into the 60s; but the modernization of the carriages and their replacement by open-plan cars on American lines meant that there was no longer anywhere to put them. Even first-class carriages which still retain individual compartments have no use for panel prints; perhaps they seem out of place in this modern, materialist world.

External decoration on carriages and railcars consisted mainly of destination boards bearing the names of the termini and sometimes intermediary points on the line. These consisted of long, narrow strips of painted wood and were affixed below the eaves or rainstrips on carriages and cars. The smallest ones fitted in metal brackets above windows, but the larger and more elaborate ones were sometimes bolted to the carriage sides. The most desirable examples are the early hand-painted variety with richly gilded lettering against the company colours. By 1890, however, trains in the United States and Canada were beginning to use enamelled metal strips for this purpose, and this custom soon spread to Europe.

There was a large variety of smaller signs, painted on wood and later enamelled on iron sheet or die-struck on brass and bronze alloys, both explanatory and minatory, and an array of such signs, mounted on a wooden board, can be most attractive as well as telling us something about customs and habits of the past. Relatively modern signs of this type tend to be rather curt, but nineteenth-century signs were often quite verbose. Often they reflect the problems of the companies in trying to educate their customers to the proper etiquette required of rail travel. While the railroads of North America thoughtfully provided brass or copper spittoons (decorated with the company crest) for the benefit of those passengers who liked a 'chaw', British companies were obsessed with the dangers of consumption and other, often unspecified diseases and put signs in the carriages, such as 'Please do not spit in the Carriage. It is offensive to other Passengers and is stated by the Medical Profession to be a source of Serious Disease'. The London, Brighton and South Coast Railway went much further with its enamelled carriage signs headed boldly 'Prevention of Consumption', followed by 'Passengers are expressly requested to refrain from the dangerous and objectionable habit of SPITTING'. Perhaps the London and South Coast lines got a much poorer quality of passenger than the other companies, since they seem to have provided warning signs and notices on all manner of bad habits and human foibles. Perhaps it was their proximity to the Continent (and the Englishman's inherent apprehension of foreigners) that prompted such notices as the trilingual warning (in English, French and German) by the South-East and Chatham Railway: 'Passengers are specially cautioned not to play Cards with strangers in the Trains.'

The permanent way

Locomotives and trains represent the more glamorous aspect of railways to the general public, few, if any, ever sparing a thought for the permanaent way without which the trains could never function. To the rail enthusiast, however, the track itself is the source of many interesting and varied items.

The combination of weight and speed means that the railroad track must be a scientifically balanced combination of materials and factors. The base consists of the ballast of gravel, stones, cinders and soil. On this rests the sleepers or ties of timber, properly seasoned, of the right type and nowadays chemically treated to prolong its life. The rails are laid on the ties and have to be secured by an elaborate scheme of chairs or tie-plates, anchors or anti-creepers, spikes and trenails. As has already been mentioned, there was a great deal of experimentation in the first decade of the railways before satisfactory iron rails were evolved. The wrought-iron rails evolved in the 1840s had a life of about twenty-five years, but by the 1870s in any case heavier loads and faster locomotives had begun to shorten the life of tracks of more recent vintage. Rails were showing considerable signs of wear after only ten years, and in some extreme cases in areas of very dense traffic they needed to be replaced almost every year.

In the 1870s, therefore, there was a renewed wave of experimentation on both sides of the Atlantic which resulted in compound rails of wrought iron clad in steel and finally the all-steel rail. Controversy continued, however, to rage over the merits of different types of rail. In the United States, Canada, Mexico and Germany the Vignoles or flange rail was preferred since it was the simplest to lay. These rails had a broad flange on the underside which was secured through tie-plates direct to the ties or sleepers. In France and Britain the double-headed rail secured in massive iron chairs was preferred.

Sections of rails used in Britain in the mid-19th century. The lower one is the combined sleeper-chair rail designed for Brunel's Great Western Railway.

47

Though more expensive to lay, this type of rail had the advantage that when the upper side began to wear out the rail could be lifted and turned over. The advent of the all-steel rail minimized the doubtful advantages of the bull-headed and double-headed rails, and gradually the flange rail became universal. The bull-headed rail could not be reversed like the double-head, though it was thought to be much stronger. It was widely used in Scotland and Ireland and survived in the latter country well into this century. A curiosity was the bridge-rail devised by Isambard Kingdom Brunel and used for many years on the Great Western Railway, using special fang bolts and square fish-plates.

Even after they became obsolete on the permanent way, old rails found many other uses in bridges and roof-beams and because of their durability they have survived in considerable quantities. Nowadays it is possible to make do with a small cross-section of rail, just sufficient to show its salient features. The fish-plates which joined the rails and the tie-plates securing flange rails often have the initials of the iron foundry, locomotive works or rail company, and some specimens even bear a date. The massive cast-iron chairs used with double-headed rails weighed anything from 15 kg to 25 kg and varied considerably in shape and design. Some had oak 'seats' on which the rails rested, and the width of the space for the rail ranged from 4 in (for lightly worked branch lines) to 8 in (for high-density main lines). The chairs were secured to the sleepers by massive iron spikes. On some lines, such as the South-Eastern Railway and the London and South-Western Railway, compound fasteners in which the spike was driven into a hollow trenail were used. Spikes of various sizes were used to secure the flange rails in America and Canada, oak keys were employed to fasten double-headed rails to the chairs, and for many years distinctive iron spikes and fish-bolts, pioneered in New South Wales, were used on many of the Australian state railways.

A problem which has long taxed the ingenuity of railroad constructors is the liability of wooden ties or sleepers to decay. In 1846 a Mr H. Greaves invented a spherical or bowl sleeper of cast iron, and wrought-iron transverse sleepers were adopted in Belgium in 1862. Similar experiments – many of them unsatisfactory – were conducted in France, Portugal and Germany in the ensuing years, but only the Vautherin sleeper, installed on the Lyons Railway in 1864, proved successful. Since then various forms of steel tie have been evolved and are to be found mainly in tropical countries.

Countries such as Canada and the United States with vast timber resources continued to use wooden ties, but at the beginning of this century the replacement rate was giving cause for alarm. By 1900 there were over a billion ties on American railroad tracks and some thirty-five to forty million of them were needing to be replaced annually. Experiments with different hardwoods, the treatment of

Silver spade presented in 1894 to Lady Northcote after she cut the first sod on the Exeter, Teign and Chagford Railway, England

timber with creosote and other preparations, and variations in the composition of the ballast were accompanied by the marking of all new ties by a special nail whose head bore the last two digits of the year. By using date-nails it soon became apparent which types of wood deteriorated most rapidly. Experiments of this sort continued into the 30s, and the date-nails have since become prized collector's items.

Apart from the everyday objects associated with the permanent way there are a number of articles which on account of their special nature have long been eminently collectable. The passage of an Act of Parliament enabling work on a new line to begin was a great occasion. The ceremony that attended the cutting of the first sod on the proposed track was an occasion attended with great pomp. For the occasion the rail companies often produced a handsome wheel-barrow with ornate carving on the sides and handles and a silver spade for the use of the dignitary performing the ceremony. These ornamental barrows and spades were usually engraved with an inscription commemorating the event. Quite a few of these relics are now in museums but many of them are still in the hands of the descendants of chairmen and directors of the old companies or the landowners whose co-operation was so vital to the passage of the railway. Other objects of this nature include silver pointing-trowels, silver-mounted mauls and hammers. The completion of a line was an even greater occasion, and for this event the last spike to be hammered home might be of silver or silver plate. Few lines went so far as to use a golden spike – as did the Transcontinental Railroad in 1869 – but generally they provided special sledge-hammers with silver mounts suitably engraved.

Alongside the permanent way were the trackside plates consisting mainly of signs and signals intended for the guidance of the engine-driver and guard or train captain. Many of these signs are cryptic to the uninitiated, bearing numerals, letters and various conventional symbols regarding gradient, speed restrictions and distances. These signs were usually of painted cast metal with raised lettering picked out in contrasting colours, usually black on white. Other wayside signs might include oval boundary marks bearing the initials of the railway company or more explicit signs inscribed 'Whistle', 'Beware of Catch Points' or 'Shut off Steam'.

Other signs along the track were intended for the general public. The great majority of them relate to trespass or the limitations of

The original Golden Spike which symbolically linked America by rail. It is now preserved in the Union Pacific Railroad Museum.

public access to the track, or the restriction of foot-bridges and paths to railway personnel. Others were mounted on the approach road to bridges over railway lines and advised of weight or speed restrictions. Many of these signs, of course, are to be found *in situ* to this day. Others have long since been consigned to the scrap-heap and reflect something of the impact which the coming of the railways meant to rural districts. One charming specimen now in the National Railway Museum at York states that 'Men employed by Farmers must not cross the main lines to fetch milk cans'.

Signalling equipment

The earliest trains operated without any form of signalling at all. In America the first railroads even had a man on horseback riding down the track in front of the locomotive to clear the way of obstruction. Even when lines became busier there tended to be a 'free-for-all' element, especially on lines with single-track working. When two locomotives approached on the same track, one of them had to reverse to the nearest side-track to allow the other to pass, and this often led to scenes of angry confrontation involving not only train crews but their passengers as well.

In the 1830s the railways of England began using rudimentary systems of flags and discs mounted on poles, and various codes were devised so that some measure of control could be enforced. The first semaphore signalling equipment was erected by Sir Charles Hutton

Painted wooden board giving a dire warning to early railway vandals; British, South-Eastern and Chatham Railway, *c.* 1863

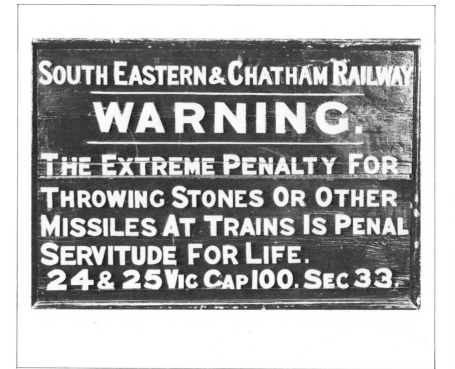

Portable spirit stove and tea-brewing kit, Drew's patent, mid-19th century

Patent candle-lights and candle-holders which provided illumination to travellers in the mid-19th century

Gregory at New Cross station in 1841 and was an adaptation of a system of signalling used by the army and navy since the days of the Napoleonic Wars. These semaphores were fitted with two signalling arms, and many different types, shapes and colour combinations may be found. Signal arms were generally of painted wood until about 1930 when sheet metal gradually came into use. Many of these signals also bore painted discs or large letters, such as S indicating a shunting signal. The more elaborate signal arms were fitted with double glass 'spectacles' which had filters of different colours, and these are now highly prized. By the 1870s, when trains running at night were becoming more common, combinations of lights were incorporated in the signals, generally a white light for safety, a blue or green light for caution and a red light for danger. Where only two lights were used, green and red were the colours employed. The first signals were always manually operated – someone had actually to go and alter the positions of the arms by hand – but in 1846 the first remote-control signals were erected at Meadowbank near Edinburgh, the arms being worked by wires from a signal-box. Within a decade distant-signals as they were then called became a standard fixture in many British and European signalling systems. They were effective only up to a distance of half a mile. The poles and gantries on which these signals were mounted were often decorated with wrought iron and had an ornamental cast-iron finial on top. Complete poles are exceptionally rare outside museums, but the decorative caps are more frequently met with.

As lines became more complex a simple visual signalling system was quite inadequate. This led to the development of various block systems which combined visual signals with the electric telegraph. In the 1880s variations of this included the permissive system and the absolute block system and culminated in the interlocking system used at busy junctions and stations. The collectables associated with these signalling systems are a vast field in themselves, ranging from the

Above Sykes' signalling instrument, patented in 1872. It was a means of interlocking the instruments with relevant levers in the signal-box, together with a form of control from the trains themselves, London, Brighton and South Coast Railway

Left Portable telegraph instrument used by officials of the Union Pacific Railroad Company in emergencies only

Opposite Uniform buttons of the British railway companies, ranging from the ornate armorial designs of the late 19th century of the severely functional designs of the London and North-Eastern Railway in the 1930s

original block instrument devised by C. V. Walker in 1850, the pegger and non-pegger instruments of the late nineteenth century and early magneto telephones of the 1890s to the complex electronic and transistorized devices of more recent years. The early block instruments, telegraphs, bells and repeaters with their brightly polished brass and wooden cases have great visual appeal. Later instruments with bakelite and proto-plastic fittings and japanned metal casing may be less attractive but often incorporate technical features of great interest.

Horns and whistles are among the more personal forms of signalling used. The copper or brass horns used by enginemen and shunters in the early years of the railways were modelled on the hunting-horns of an earlier generation. A great favourite in the 1880s was the Lusty type which emitted a hearty blast as its name suggests. Pocket whistles come in an immense variety since they were used by guards and conductors, look-out men, pilotmen and station-masters the world over. Signalling flags offer less scope since they were restricted to a few basic colours, and here again red and green soon became universally accepted.

Even the insulators on the telegraph wires along the permanent way are not without considerable interest. The earliest examples were produced in stoneware, ironstone, porcelain and other hard-wearing ceramic materials and often bear the manufacturer's name or initials, the date and sometimes the name of the railway company.

Magnetic telephone used by British railway companies in the late 19th century

By the end of the nineteenth century glass insulators were coming into use and they may be found in many shades and tints of clear or opaque glass, again with names, initials, dates and serial numbers on them.

Large and often highly ornate lamps were attached to level-crossing gates and signal-boxes. The name boards from signal-boxes were of cast iron with raised lettering, occasionally of brass, though more often of painted wood. Enamelled iron signs were also used increasingly from 1900 onwards. Many of these signs and boards have come on to the market in recent years with the closure of so many lines, and this has stimulated interest in what was a rather neglected field.

Station furniture and equipment

Railway stations are almost as old as railways themselves, and in the past century and a half have made a major contribution to the world's architecture. The great stations of the world, like New York's Grand Central, the Gare du Nord in Paris, the Hauptbahnhof in Leipzig and St Pancras in London, are important landmarks and triumphs of engineering but they lack the atmosphere of the small country stations, many of which are still in use. Many of the old-time companies had their own distinctive, and often bizarre, ideas of what a rural station should look like, resulting in incongruities such as Tudor cottages in the Prairies and baroque castles in the Scottish Highlands, but that was all part of their charm. The station was frequently the most important building in a village and in countries where the railroad opened up virgin territory it was often the focal point around which the settlement developed. From an early date the station often incorporated the function of a telegraph office, and many a country station-master was also the local postmaster, being indeed the custodian of all forms of transport and communication in his area.

Rationalization and modernization have taken their toll of the rural stations. Even where lines still exist many of the stations along the route have been closed, and the buildings are either derelict or have been razed to the ground. Paradoxically many of the stations and signal-boxes in areas where lines are now defunct have been preserved and converted into private houses. British Rail did a brisk trade in the 1960s selling off obsolete stations (which often included an existing station-master's house of some substance), and some of them have been restored by their owners and converted into private museums of railwayana.

The closure of so many stations in Britain and America in particular has brought a vast amount of collectable material on to the market. The station name boards from obscure hamlets, halts and sidings, often with quaint names to match, are the most desirable, but

A selection of railway guards' whistles in metal, wood and ivory; British, late 19th century

many collectors have endeavoured to acquire boards from stations with some sentimental attachment.

The name boards of cast metal with raised lettering were produced in several sizes from the large size mounted prominently on the platform or the trackside to the small signs screwed to the backs of benches and the sides of buildings. The amalgamation of companies, the regrouping and later political changes which affected the railways in many countries were not always reflected in station signs, many of which continued to display the insignia and initials of obsolete formations and were often replaced only when they wore out. I can recall a station in the present-day German Democratic Republic where the Communist authorities had not yet got around to changing a sign incorporating the word *Reichsbahn,* which went back beyond both Hitler and the Weimar Republic to the days of the Kaiser. In Britain, for example, many of the old company signs from the pre-grouping era were retained in the 30s and 40s and only scrapped after nationalization in 1948 when British Rail adopted plain enamelled sheet metal signs in the standard regional colours.

Station names were also featured in the cast-iron crossbars of the lamp-posts, though this practice was confined to the larger stations. As a rule the name found on station fixtures was that of the company, often in an abbreviated form, and followed the same pattern as that found on the trains themselves. In this category come the fittings from lavatories, waiting-rooms, restaurants and bars, ticket-offices and booking-halls, and their interest depends largely on the badges and inscriptions found on them.

Next to name boards the most collectable items are probably the lamps and lanterns which illuminated the station and its yard. Like the lamps used on the trains, there were many varieties, from the magnificent hanging oil-lamps used in station foyers and waiting-rooms to the candle-lanterns attached to wall-sconces. Wall clocks from waiting-rooms and booking-halls are much in demand. Horologically they were sturdy and dependable – they had to be since the public relied on them so much – but from an early date were strictly functional in appearance. Relatively few of them had an inscription on their dial but those which have engraved or enamelled inscriptions relating to individual companies are highly prized. The old key-wind clocks were superseded in the 20s by more accurate electric timepieces, but there are still a few of the ancient wall clocks with their familiar octagonal case in service. My own local station has a magnificent and venerable grandfather clock mounted on the wall – on which I cast the most covetous of eyes every time I pass it!

Most of the remaining station waiting-rooms are now equipped with some form of central heating, but not so long ago the roaring log or coal fire was a cheery sight on a cold winter's day. Relics from those days include the massive wrought-iron or beaten-copper fenders, burnished brass scuttles or japanned coal-boxes, and the presence of a company name or initials makes them much more desirable.

Apart from the dining-cars on the trains, restaurants, buffets and refreshment rooms have long been a feature of many depots and stations, varying enormously in quality and service, from line to line and country to country. Although paper plates and cups and throwaway plastic cutlery have been introduced as labour-saving devices in many countries, the good old-fashioned crockery and cutlery is still around. Cups, saucers and various sizes of plates bearing railway insignia may be encountered, but seldom will the collector encounter anything quite so lavish as the brightly decorated plates provided by some of the American and Canadian companies. Some of them even provided plates with fairy-tale and nursery-rhyme motifs for the use of the very youngest diners.

Larger items include electroplated serving dishes, platters, coffee pots, bowls and even tureens and meat covers with embossed and enamelled crests. Knives, forks and spoons bearing the initials and emblems of the railway companies, being less prone to damage, have survived in larger quantities than the crockery, and an impressive array can still be assembled for a reasonable outlay. Cutlery, crockery and even table linen bearing company crests and initials were used not only in the station restaurants but also in the railway dining-cars and often in the hotels operated by the companies.

Apart from name boards there are many signs associated with stations. The early signs were comparatively verbose and certainly left the reader in no doubt as to their meaning. One must remember that at the time they were current the railway was a new phenomenon and the public had to be re-educated accordingly. The railway companies were most particular about the use of their facilities, judging by some of the signs now displayed in the National Railway Museum, York. A common notice in the days before the internal combustion engine read: 'None but Company's horses allowed to drink at this Trough.'

Toilet facilities at stations were also restricted, as the Cheshire Lines intimated: 'These closets are intended for the convenience of passengers only, workmen, cabmen, fishporters and idlers are not permitted to use them. BY ORDER.' The Companies applied a very strict code of conduct to the general public, to people who while not in company employment depended none the less on the railway for their livelihood and, of course, to the railway personnel themselves. The men who drove cabs to and from the station were singled out in this notice displayed at stations of the South-Eastern and Chatham Railway: 'Any Cabman skylarking or otherwise mis-conducting himself on the Managing Committee's premises or Smoking whilst his Cab is standing alongside the Platform will be required to leave the Station immediately.' The Great Central Railway displayed a brass and black enamel notice with this exhortation: 'When answer-

Pair of Great Western Railway brass candle-lights, with pierced and finial-led tops; late 19th century

57

Indian Tree pattern cream jug used by the Pullman Company of America

ing public telephone calls Company servants must reply in the most courteous manner and must not rest content until they feel they have satisfied the applicant by giving him the fullest information in their power.'

These are the gems of railway antiques, but there are countless examples of more perfunctory notices which were just as useful. Signs in carved wood, cast brass, enamelled iron, plastic and etched glass forbidding this, explaining that or merely indicating lavatories, refreshment rooms and waiting-rooms may be found in every language under the sun, with the occasional addition of conventional symbols (for the illiterate) and the name, initials or emblem of the railway company.

The mundane equipment of the station-master's office and the booking-hall yields many items of interest. Old telephones of the stick type are fairly plentiful, but much rarer are the scissors telephones, clamped to a wall bracket with a collapsible arm which could be extended as required. Early cradle telephones with handsome brass or nickel rests are also in great demand. From the very beginning the railway companies were enthusiastic paper-pushers, and it is incredible to contemplate now the vast amount of form-filling required of railway officials in the handling of a single parcel. The ephemera associated with railway bureaucracy is discussed in Chapter 8, but there are more substantial items connected with the paperwork.

Every station-master and booking-clerk had an impressive array of brass and rubber stamps, some with movable date-slugs and others incorporating enumerating devices which covered a wide variety of purposes connected with passenger and freight traffic. Many of these stamps bore the name or initials of the company; others had the name of the line or even the name of the depot or station. The combinations of inscription possible are almost infinite. Security was always a watchword of the railways, and there was frequent resort to sealing wax to secure packets containing valuable company documents, tickets, vouchers, remittances and the like. Every station-master, therefore, had his own distinctive seal, and these often bore the coat of arms in addition to the name of the company and perhaps also the name of the station. Unbroken specimens of the wax impressions from these seals turn up from time to time as caches of old railway documents are unearthed but they are best kept on the entire envelope or wrapper if possible. Relatively few of the actual seals themselves ever come on the market and they are invariably eagerly snapped up. A charming custom of some of the old railway companies when they absorbed their smaller competitors was to mount their seals and matrices in an ornamental table-top under glass. Such tables, salvaged from the directors' boardrooms of the companies which, themselves, have long since disappeared, are among the most treasured rarities of railway antiques today.

Apart from the seals there were small spirit lamps and various patent devices with wicks and tapers enclosed in silver or brass cases. Pocket sealing kits, complete with stick of wax and minuscule candlestick, are worth hunting for, especially if the leather or shagreen case bears the crest or monogram of old railway companies.

On the subject of security one must not forget the many different forms of lock and padlock used by station staff. They range from the massive padlocks used on gates and doors to the tiny locks fitted to switches and money-boxes. Both the locks and the keys that operated them were often decorated with the company's mark, and this adds considerably to their variety.

The earliest tickets (see Chapter 4) were either torn or cancelled in pen and ink by the inspector, ticket-collector or conductor, but after the introduction of the more compact pasteboard ticket in 1837 a more satisfactory method of defacing the surface was required. Americans claim that the ticket-punch was invented by conductors on the Erie Railway, but the British give credit to William Carson of Creetown in Scotland, who was ever after known as 'Tickety' Carson. It may have been no small coincidence that the inventor of the pasteboard ticket, Thomas Edmondson, worked just across the

A range of railway signs on display at the National Railway Museum, York, England

Solway Firth on the Newcastle and Carlisle Railway. The earliest punches made a plain circular hole in the ticket, but later punches became much more sophisticated, cutting an infinite variety of holes. Others indented the surface without cutting, and embossed letters, numerals and symbols whose code was frequently changed for security reasons. By means of these distinctive punches ticket-collectors and inspectors could tell at a glance whether a ticket had been used on a single continuous journey, whether that journey had been broken (perhaps illegally), and whether the punch marks tallied with the date stamped on the ticket at the time of issue. Thus each company might have a large number of different punches at any one time, and over the years the variety of punches might run into hundreds. There was a great deal of variation in the shape of heads and handles and considerable scope in decorative features, so punches themselves constitute one of the major collecting fields.

Among the miscellaneous items found in glass, porcelain, pewter, brass, iron and nickel-plate are ashtrays from offices and waiting-rooms, embossed or engraved with company motifs, urns for dispensing hot or cold drinks – a feature of many stations in eastern Europe and Asia where drinking water may be suspect – and inkstands and inkwells. Massive cast-iron paperweights with leather pads on their base may be encountered with railway insignia. Even rulers, pens and pencils were marked to indicate that they were the property of the company and thus qualify for inclusion among railway antiques. Even such ordinary items as penknives and scissors are of interest it they are clearly identified as belonging to the railway, though few examples are as elaborate as the scissors and matching case in silver and gold with crest and ornamental lettering that were used to cut the tape at opening ceremonies.

Miscellaneous items

Among the miscellaneous items of rail equipment the most important are the cans in iron, aluminium, copper, brass, japanned or enamelled metal with company insignia used for many purposes. The most desirable are the oilcans which may be found with disproportionately long narrow spouts and range from tall cylinders to squat cone shapes. Many of them had patent pouring or regulating devices, and the inclusion of these features is an important plus factor. Other distinctive cans were used for water, kerosene, paraffin, grease and paste. On a more personal level were the lunch pails and boxes used by railmen and, tiniest of all, the pay tins which date back to the days when wages were paid in gold and silver rather than the paper to which we are now accustomed. These tins were small cylinders in which railmen collected their money each week. Each tin bore the man's name or works' number, and the shape and composition of these tins varied from company to company.

Elaborate seal used by the Edinburgh Suburban and Southside Junction Railway Company, 1880

Miscellaneous office equipment of the Chicago and Eastern Illinois Railroad: spirit lamp, sealing wax, wax sealer and money envelope with wax seal impression

Davies and Tourtel patent Electric Reading Lamp, operated by a penny in the slot and leased to British railway companies by the Railway Electric Light Syndicate, *c.* 1900

Right Pistol used for warning signals, and bearing the mark of the Great Northern Railway; British, 19th century

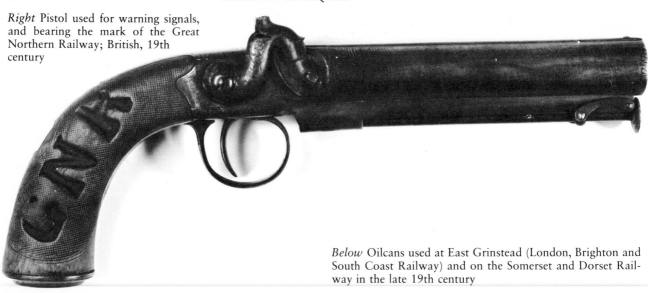

Below Oilcans used at East Grinstead (London, Brighton and South Coast Railway) and on the Somerset and Dorset Railway in the late 19th century

Apart from the lunch boxes carried by the railmen the more enterprising companies often sold packed meals to passengers in an era before refreshment rooms or dining-cars were widespread. The simplest types contained sandwiches and buns alone, but the more elaborate ones had compartments for salt, pepper, butter, mustard and cheese, and there were even lunch baskets for hire, complete with tiny kettle and spirit stove.

Station control and security includes a number of collectable items from megaphones to warning pistols, not to mention the paraphernalia associated with station guards and railway police. Grim relics of World War II are the Air Raid Precautions and Civil Defence equipment allocated to stations and depots in many European countries, but even in peace-time many companies maintained fire-fighting equipment, from helmets to axes, which adds yet another dimension to rail relics.

The health of railway personnel was of paramount importance, and this has yielded some interesting items from the small first-aid kits carried by the locomotive staff to the equipment used in the regular checks made on the fitness of drivers and guards. Various ingenious devices have been used at different times by the old railway companies to test the eyesight and colour-blindness of their staff.

Finally one should not overlook the everyday tools of the railmen's trade, the fireman's shovel, the wheeltapper's hammer and the shunter's pole, all of which had their vital role to play but are now largely things of the past.

Pay tins and a station cash bag, Caledonian and Great Central Railways

Women were first employed by the railways during World War I: a lady ticket-collector on the London and South-Western Railway *c.* 1916

3 Railway uniforms

Railway collectors have shown comparatively little interest until now in complete uniforms, and this is a matter for some regret since few examples of the earliest coats, tunics and trousers of rail personnel have survived intact. The tendency is towards specialization in the minor items of uniform, the headgear, badges and buttons. As part of the Corporate Identity Programme of British Rail an entirely new style of uniform was introduced, bearing an uncanny resemblance to that worn by the erstwhile Afrika Korps – hence the nickname by which this garb has since become known. The adoption of the new-style jacket, trousers and cap brought an immense quantity of obsolete clothing on to the market at giveaway prices, and for the first time collectors, unable to pass up such a bargain, began to give some consideration to the complete uniforms in service up to 1964. Since then attention has been turned to the uniforms of earlier periods, and the magnificent frock-coats, top hats and gold-braided livery of earlier generations of railmen has appreciated considerably in value. These remarks relating to British Rail also apply to uniform of other countries. In many cases uniform, as such, was confined to headgear and armbands and offers little scope in any case; but others, notably Germany, Russia and other countries of central and eastern Europe, often had elaborate uniforms which reflected the exalted status of railway employees in the community at large.

The earliest uniforms were modelled on the scarlet and blue livery worn by coachmen of the stage-coach era. Full-length coats were worn by the locomotive crew as a protection against the wind and the weather, and top hats were reinforced with leather. Station staff had scarlet tunics with blue facings, blue trousers with red stripes and a superabundance of gold braid everywhere. The scarlet livery, however, was ill-suited to the sulphurous fumes, the soot and grime in the Steam Age and soon gave way to more sombre, if serviceable, hues of navy blue and dark brown. Touches of colour were retained where-ever possible, and this applied to porters and ushers as well as ticket-collectors, inspectors and station-masters at the depots and to the conductors, train captains, guards and stewards on the trains. Staff who were exposed to the more dirty and dangerous jobs were equipped with various forms of protective clothing from the grease-top caps of the locomotive engineer and fireman to the stout leather

Dress uniform of a Group 'A', first-class station-master, Great Western Railway, c. 1930

Right The staff of an unidentified British station about 1860—station-master, booking-clerk, guard, porter and messenger boy—showing the variety of uniforms then in use

Porter's cap and cap badges of brakeman and conductor on the Great Northern Railway, America

or canvas leggings of the vanmen and brakemen. The jackets, trousers, tunics and overalls of the locomen were produced in tarpaulin, canvas, denim and other hard-wearing materials and were used until they simply wore out. Consequently they are now quite scarce, though there is as yet little demand compared with the more attractive depot, station and train uniforms.

A surprising variety of headgear has been worn by railway personnel all round the world in the past century and a half. The stylish top hats, stove-pipes and beavers of the mid-nineteenth century were decorated with silk ribbons and braids, sometimes embroidered with company names or more often the designation of the wearer. The top hat survived as part of the station-master's ceremonial uniform into the early part of this century, and examples are much sought after. In some countries derby and bowler hats were worn by station personnel and these sometimes bore a metal badge, but by the 1880s peaked caps of various styles were becoming the general fashion. Stylistically the American and some European companies favoured a cap with a relatively tall side and a small diameter across the top. The British companies had caps with a shallower peak and a broader top, and the Russian and German railways opted for caps which followed contemporary military lines with comparatively high fronts. Pillboxes, kepis and shakos, echoing contemporary military fashions, were used by some British companies and many of the state lines in Europe at the turn of the century, and these were often richly decked in gold lace, braid and colourful piping.

Braided bands, epaulettes and elaborate piping decorated the tunics and coats of station staff, subtle variations often indicating the different grades. Some companies favoured gold lace epaulettes and shoulder boards; others chose rings of gold lace on the tunic cuffs in the same fashion as naval officers. This penchant for fancy uniforms was especially strong in European countries where petty officials enjoyed considerable status in their community. In America, by contrast, many railroads had little or no formal uniforms for their depot and train staff, greater emphasis being placed on a badge worn prominently on the cap or jacket. By the end of the century, however, even the American companies realized the necessity for their personnel to wear clearly identifiable uniform, and quite complex regulations were then enforced, giving descriptions of the prescribed uniform down to the smallest detail.

Drivers and firemen on British and European railways wore grease-top hats with a rigid peak, whereas American engineers preferred a cloth cap, said to have been devised by an unknown fireman about 1905. In many countries railmen wore a scarf or bandana over their hair, secured by a sweatband. Invariably the colour chosen was red, the international code for danger, so that it could be used as a signal in an emergency. The same thinking lay behind the scarlet dress neckties introduced by the London and South-Western Railway in 1885; the elaborate bow could be swiftly untied and used as a warning signal if necessary.

For security reasons personnel authorized to work in certain areas, in the sidings, loco sheds, the goods yards and even on the main lines,

The staff at Wallington station, London, Brighton and South Coast Railway, *c.* 1900

London and North Western Railway
passenger guard, 1906

had to be easily identified. Every railway company had its own
system of brassards, armbands and cuff-titles in various colours with
inscriptions identifying the employee's role. These bands may be
found with such designations as Look-out Man, Pilotman, Porter,
Yardmaster, Brakeman, Vanman, Conductor, Guard, Engineman,
Inspector, Train Dispatcher and Foreman, or their equivalents in
other languages.

Badges and buttons

Among the most popular of all rail relics are the badges and buttons
which bore the company insignia. Their small size, attractive appearance and relative cheapness enable even the humblest of collectors to
put together an impressive display at no great cost, though the
emblems of the nineteenth century in general and the more obscure of
the smaller railways of this century will take some finding.

Cap badges were sometimes woven directly into the hatband but
more usually were made of metal thread and these are the most
desirable. Detachable metal badges, cast in white metal, brass or
bronze, came into general use in the late nineteenth century, though
some examples date back as far as the 1850s. The inscription and

decoration on these cap badges varied widely from company to company. Some preferred a measure of standardization with every employee wearing a badge consisting of the company crest or name. Others cloaked their identity and gave their personnel badges which merely stated their function: brakeman, driver, fireman, engineer, conductor, guard, station-master, baggage agent and trainman, as the case might be. This was a practice favoured by many American and European railways, though quite a few of them incorporated their company symbol or name, almost as an afterthought.

After World War I the ornate cast-metal cap badges gradually gave way to cheaper and more eye-catching insignia of sheet metal strips with the inscription picked out in contrasting enamel colours. The florid lettering which reached its peak at the turn of the century was superseded by the more functional styles of the Bauhaus and Gill-Sans which make the old style badges look like baroque wine labels by comparison.

Elaborate breast badges, reminiscent of the lawmen of the Wild West, were worn by personnel of many American railroads, and, indeed, there would often have been a close connection between the railroad and the forces of law and order in the bad old days when train robbery was a frequent occurrence. Many of these badges, in fact, were worn by personnel not directly employed by the railroad, such as the clerks and security officers who worked the Railway Mail Service of the United States Post Office and the agents of Wells Fargo, American Express and the Adams Company who operated express services in conjunction with the railroads.

Collar badges are relatively uncommon and took the form of company insignia and personal numbers worn on the high-necked tunics affected by personnel on many European and Asiatic railways in particular. The turned-down lapels of coats and jackets worn by railmen in many countries encouraged the use of lapel badges. Like the cap badges, these often identified the role of the employee, but greater attention always seems to have been given to their decorative aspects. As usual the company crest was a prominent feature, cast in gold, silver, brass and white metal and frequently richly enamelled. After World War I the design and construction of lapel badges universally became simpler, and there was a vogue for tin-plate and even plastic pinbacks, particularly in America. At the same time the application of cheap, multicolour lithography to these flat-surfaced badges gave rise to a vast array of motifs, many of them incorporating advertising slogans. Such pinbacks died out in the 1950s and they have since become quite elusive.

During World War I patriotic women in Britain mercilessly hounded any strapping young man in civilian clothes, handing out white feathers – the badge of the coward. To avoid a great deal of unpleasantness all round the railway companies gave their personnel distinctive enamelled badges to wear in the lapels of their jackets

Above Staff cap badges of the London, Brighton and South Coast Railway, *c.* 1900

Below Breast badge worn by a porter employed on the US Post Office Department Railway Mail Service

when off duty and out of uniform. These badges bore the national crown or coat of arms in addition to the company name and the prominent words 'Railway Service' or 'War Service' to indicate that the wearer was in fact performing work that was vital to the war effort. Each badge was serially numbered on the back, and their use was strictly controlled to prevent them getting into the wrong hands.

Belt buckles may seem an unlikely source of railway insignia, but in those countries where personnel wore belted tunics quite elaborate badges were often to be found on the clasp. Many of the old-style American companies equipped their railmen with belts whose buckles had a very large rectangular guard, and this provided great scope for decoration, following the same lines as those worn by the stage-coach drivers and guards of an earlier generation.

A wide range of insignia and pictorial motifs is to be found on the buttons of the older railway companies. The buttons themselves come in several sizes, each company favouring three or four main sizes for tunic, waistcoat, sleeve, shoulder-strap and chin-strap respectively. Buttons were produced in gilt-bronze, brass, white metal and chrome. Some European lines favoured pewter or spelter, and those in some countries of Asia and Africa used horn, bone or even wood. Bone buttons were used in Britain as a wartime economy measure, and various kinds of plastic have been used in many countries in more recent years.

Buttons varied considerably in quality even within the same company, those worn by station-masters and senior depot staff frequently being of better material and finish than those worn by porters, clerks and cleaners. Sometimes this was indicated by an inscription on the reverse, but the comparative quality is readily apparent as a rule. There were also subtle changes in the design of buttons used by a company over a period of years, and this is most noticeable in the style of lettering which tended to become plainer in the 1920s and 30s. Absorption of smaller companies might also lead to a slight change of name or initials on the buttons used by the parent company, quite apart from the disappearance of the insignia of the companies that were taken over.

Stylistically buttons followed no set pattern. Many of them dating back to the mid-nineteenth century bore no more than the company's initials, whereas the most sumptuous heraldic devices survived on the buttons of many companies well into the present century. Particularly attractive are those buttons which depicted a tiny locomotive. Among those that followed this theme were the North London, the Londonderry and Lough Swilly (Ireland), the Burma State Railway, the Dutch Railways (Hollandsche Spoorwegen Maatschappij), the Hastonville, Mantua and Fairmont Railroad, the Nashville Railway and the Philadelphia Traction Company. Southern Pacific Lines featured the sun rising over the railroad track, and the Soo Line incorporated the dollar sign. Buttons are fairly easy to

Coat lapel badges of American railroad brotherhoods and trade unions

identify since the name or initials of the company are usually inscribed, but one that often puzzles beginners is the button cryptically inscribed 'Katy', a nickname derived from the initials of the Kansas and Texas Line. Conventional symbolism is relatively uncommon. Several Irish lines used a shamrock emblem, while various kinds of crown appeared on the buttons of the Canadian National Railways and the Gold Coast General Railway. New Zealand Railways formerly used the royal cipher before opting for their present stylized logotype based on the initials NZR. British Railways used a wheel in the period immediately after nationalization, then experimented with a BR logotype in 1964–6, while searching for that elusive Corporate Identity, before evolving the present 'two-way rail' emblem.

Apart from the badges issued by the railway companies, there are many ancillary forms of identification and adornment worth considering. The lapel badges of the railmen's unions, long service pins and buttonhole badges, usually in brightly coloured enamels, have an important place in any collection of railway insignia.

Watches

Several of the items of personal equipment used by railmen, such as whistles and ticket-punches, have already been mentioned, but perhaps the most important item of all was the timepiece. From the very beginning of passenger rail services in the 1820s the importance of running the trains on time was appreciated by all rail employees from line superintendents down to the lowliest brakeman. Since traffic increased more rapidly than signalling systems could be developed, the accuracy of timekeeping became doubly important. Many of the early railway accidents were caused by trains running ahead or behind schedule and collisions arising out of this lack of synchronization.

Right Railway guard's watch made by the Hamilton Company of Lancaster, Pennsylvania, together with the decorative case for the watch inspection card

Below Railway guards' watches: (left) circular silver watch used on the Manchester, Sheffield and Lincolnshire Railway, *c.* 1890; (right) mid-19th century watch in an oblong brass case, made by George Littlewort of London for an unidentified railway company

American gold watch-cases with engraved locomotives. Though not official railroad issue, such watches are highly prized for their railway motifs.

Britain, the United States, France and Germany in particular devoted a great deal of attention to the problems of accurate timekeeping and in the 1880s developed precision watches which eventually became an indispensable part of the railman's equipment. Everyone connected with the smooth running of the trains, both on the line and at the stations and depots, carried a watch whose accuracy was checked regularly and synchronized daily at the start of each shift. Railway watches were always larger than those in ordinary use, and many unusual styles were evolved. Early British watches were mounted in a square or oblong brass case which was often decorated with company inscriptions. They were very accurate but were relatively expensive to produce, and by the end of the century the British had lost ground to the Swiss and American watchmakers who by using advanced factory techniques managed to make both cheap and accurate watches. Continental watches with the now familiar names of Longines, Vacheron, Le Coultre and Omega competed with Waterbury, Waltham, Elgin, Rockford and Hamilton in supplying the world's railways with reliable timepieces. These watches have immense appeal to the horologist on account of the names found on their movements, but the collector of railway antiques tends to pay a handsome premium for watches impressed or engraved with the names of railway companies on or inside the back cover. A word of caution, however, may not come amiss; not every watch with a very obvious railway appearance was actually used by railmen. A number of less than scrupulous watchmakers, especially in America, marketed watches with pictures of locomotives on their dials or engraved on their cases, or gave them impressive names such as the Railway Special. Quite often such watches will be found to be technically inferior. Yet for all that they have a certain period charm which has endeared them to collectors.

ALGOMA CENTRAL & HUDSON BAY RAILWAY
COMMERCIAL TRAVELLERS' TICKET
GOOD FOR ONE FIRST CLASS PASSAGE

From *Steelton*
To *Michipicoten*

Commencing on date of issue and subject to conditions of COMMERCIAL TRAVELLERS' CERTIFICATE No.

NO STOP-OVER ALLOWED   NOT TRANSFERABLE

FORM
C. T. 5   14938
Traffic Manager

CHICAGO & WESTERN INDIANA R.R.
25 RIDE TICKET
—BETWEEN—
ROSELAND
—AND—
CHICAGO
Good only on C. & W. I. R. R. Suburban Trains. Not good unless within one year from date of sale.
THE TWENTY-FIFTH RIDE IS REPRESENTED BY THE BODY OF THIS TICKET TO BE TAKEN UP BY CONDUCTOR.

Form T 7
17-0

24 23 22 21 20 19 18 17 16
15 14 13 12 11 10 9 8 7 6 5 4 3 2

C.&W.I.R.R.
Accounting Dept. Check
FIRST RIDE
—BETWEEN—
ROSELAND
—AND—
CHICAGO
NOT GOOD IF DETACHED
25 RIDE TICKET
Form T 7
17-0

FEMALE ★   Lackawanna Railroad   Delaware, Lackawanna & Western R.R.   MALE ★
5   Agent will punch ★ following the word MALE or FEMALE to describe sex
12-TRIP WEEKLY COMMUTATION TICKET
For the exclusive use of the person whose personal signature must be affixed below in ink or indelible pencil before ticket is good for passage
M
To 12 Continuous Trips Between
ORANGE and NEW YORK
This Ticket is also valid for passage between New York and Athenia or Glen Ridge
Good only from SUNDAY to SATURDAY of Week Ending
NOT GOOD
AFTER SATURDAY
L 12
Subject to Rules Shown on Back
Passenger Traffic Manager
12 11 10 9 8 7 6 5 4 3 2 1
★ ★ ★ ★ ★ ★ ★ ★ ★ ★ ★ ★

DES MOINES & CENTRAL IOWA R. R.
40-RIDE SCHOOL TICKET
Good only between points shown on cover.
Not Good If Detached   Form Com. 2.
from Book.
10068   V. P. & G. M.

VIRGINIA & TRUCKEE RAILWAY
Good for One Continuous First-Class Passage
RENO
—TO—
CARSON CITY
On conditions named in contract and worthless if detached.
Form 112 Special Ex.   NEVADA DIAMOND JUBILEE Celebration
Void if Detached
730
IF FOR HALF ½ PUNCH HERE

NEW YORK CENTRAL
RAILROAD   100
NEW YORK, N. Y. to
CINCINNATI, O.
Good for One Passage in PULLMAN CARS on payment of charges for space occupied.
Limited to ONE (1) YEAR in addition to date stamped on back. Subject to tariff regulations.
Not Transferable.
Gen. Pass. Traffic Mgr.

NEW YORK CENTRAL
& HUDSON RIVER RAILROAD.
Good for One Continuous Passage
BUFFALO to NIAGARA FALLS
SPECIAL ONE DAY EXCURSION TICKET.
To be taken on the day of sale at indicated passenger Agents at stations. Not good on Mich. Cent. R. R. Trains.
This ticket is valid only when attached to its coupon. Signature, and is subject to conditions printed thereon.
87
371 RT   Not good on Limited Trains.   390

Algoma Central & Hudson Bay R'y.
Special Excursion Ticket
GOING COUPON ONE PASSAGE
SAULT STE. MARIE, ONT.
TO
Kan
Not Good After ___ 3. 19
NOT TRANSFERABLE
NO STOP-OVER ALLOWED THIS TICKET VOID IF DETACHED
Form 2   35740

VIRGINIA & TRUCKEE RAILWAY
Non-Transferable Special Excursion Ticket
Account
Nevada Diamond Jubilee
Celebration
Good for One Continuous First-Class Passage
CARSON CITY
—TO—
RENO
Subject to the following Contract and Conditions:
1st. Going Trip. Not good unless date of sale is stamped on back and good only for continuous passage leaving on Oct. 30th and 31st, 1939.
2nd. Return Trip. Must be completed prior to midnight of Oct. 31, 1939.
3rd. Stop-overs. Will not be allowed on either going or return trip.
4th. Baggage. Will not be received or checked hereon.
5th. Alterations. This ticket is void if the coupons are detached from contract or if any alterations or erasures are made hereon.
FORM 112
Special Excursion
P.T.M.
730
IF FOR HALF ½ PUNCH HERE

CANADIAN PACIFIC RAILWAY
Via Direct Line
ONE PASSAGE
WINNIPEG DEPOT Man.
—TO—
NORTH TRANSCONA Man.
LIMIT: ONE YEAR
Stop-overs allowed
NOT TRANSFERABLE.
Pass'r Traffic Manager
COACH   00019

PASSENGER'S
SOUVENIR TICKET
NOT GOOD FOR PASSAGE
ISSUED BY
VIRGINIA & TRUCKEE RAILWAY
FROM
RENO, NEVADA
—TO—
CARSON CITY, NEVADA
and return
Account
NEVADA DIAMOND JUBILEE CELEBRATION
OCTOBER 29, 30, 31, 1939
730

The HISTORIC V. & T. RAILWAY
THIS railroad of standard gauge, was built (and equipped) between Virginia City, Nevada, and Reno, Nevada, (52 miles) in 1869-1870, at a cost of five million dollars, primarily to serve the Mines, Mills and the Comstock District generally.
I. E. James surveyed 21 mile route from Virginia City to Carson City in 24 days.
Construction commenced in March, 1869, with James as chief engineer, diverting 1,600 workers of 58 construction camps.
September 28, 1869, drove silver spike into the first tie, and was the first superintendent of the V. & T.
Three Baldwin locomotives hauled from Reno to Carson through Washoe Valley. Two Baldwin locomotives hauled from Reno over steep Geiger grade to Virginia City.
First train from Carson City to Virginia City on January 29, 1870.

GRAND TRUNK R'Y.
Industrial Fair and Agricultural Exposition, SEPT. 4TH to 16TH, 1893.
TORONTO
—TO—
Exhibition Grounds and Ret.
Good only for passage each way on date of issue. Not transferable.
2253

NASHVILLE CHATTANOOGA & ST. LOUIS RAIL WAY. ISSUED BY
TENNESSEE TICKET CLAIM COUPON
To be retained by passenger. Not good for passage
The Nashville, Chattanooga & St. Louis Railway has on the date stamped hereon received for a ticket, of same form and number as this coupon, the rate designated in its tariff now in effect for intra-state travel wholly within the State of Tennessee from
Bell Buckle to Nashville
This coupon is issued to the purchaser of the ticket as evidence that the bearer hereof is entitled to collect weekly and also under the conditions of an order promulgated by the Railroad Commission of Tennessee dated February 15, 1908, the excess, if any, of the amount received by said railway for said ticket over the amount which would have been received had said ticket been sold at rate of two and one-half cents a mile.
If under the provisions of said order this coupon should become payable, it may be surrendered to the General Passenger agent or to any ticket agent of this company, who shall forward it to the General Pass'r Agent for payment through said ticket agent.
A copy of said order is posted at all of this company's passenger stations in Tennessee.
1st Cond'r
punch here
TENN.   Local.   Gen'l Pass. Agent
715

NEW YORK, ONTARIO and WESTERN RAILWAY COMPANY

	HALF O FARE		Walton (Br'ge St)	
★ New York			Colchester	★
★ Weehawken	BOOK No.	TICKET No.	Hawleys	★
★	A 7454	100	Hamden	★
★ Cornwall	Form C		De Lancy	★
★ Firthcliffe	Southern Division		Delhi	★
★ Meadow Brook			Phillipsport	★
★ Rock Tavern			Spring Glen	★
★ Burnside			Ellenville	★
★ Campbell Hall			Napanoch	★
★ Crystal Run			Wawarsing	★
★ Middletown			Kerhonkson	★
★ Fair Oaks			Accord	★
★ Winterton			Kyserike	★
★ High View			High Falls	★
★ Mamakating			Cottekill	★
★ Summitville			Hurley	★
★ Mountain Dale			Kingston	★
★ Woodridge			Wurtsboro	★
★ Fallsburgh			Haven	★
★ Luzon			Westbrookville	★
★ Ferndale			Por i Orange	★
★ Liberty			Cuddebackville	★
★ Parksville			Valley Junction	★
★ Livingston Manor			Oakland	★
★ Hazel			Hartwood	★
★ Roscoe			St. Joseph's	★
★ Cook's Falls			Monticello	★
★ Hortons			JANUARY	
★ Chiloway			FEBRUARY	
★ Elk Brook			MARCH	
★ Trout Brook			APRIL	
★ East Branch			MAY	
★ Fish's Eddy			JUNE	
★ Cadosia			JULY	
★ Apex			AUGUST	
★ Rock Rift			SEPTEMBER	
★ Bearston			OCTOBER	
★ Walton			NOVEMBER	
★ Westbrook			DECEMBER	
★ Northfield			1941	
★ Merrickville			1942	
★ Franklin			1943	
★ Maywood			1944	
★ Youngs			1945	
★ South Unadilla			1946	
★ Sidney			1947	
★			1948	
★			NORTH	
★			SOUTH	
Not Redeemable				
if Punched Here	1 2 3 4 5 6 7 8 9 10			
	11 12 13 14 15 16 17			
	18 19 20 21 22 23 24			
	25 26 27 28 29 30 31			

RAND McNALLY & COMPANY, NEW YORK

LOWVILLE & BEAVER RIVER
RAILROAD COMPANY.
Good only for One Continuous Passage
NEW BREMEN to LOWVILLE
To be begun within THIRTY (30) days from day of sale, and stamped on back hereof by Company's Agent. In addition to extended time within which journey may be begun, holder hereof assumes Railroad Company from all liability as to baggage for wearing apparel not exceeding in value $100.
9231
General Manager

LOWVILLE & BEAVER RIVER
RAILROAD COMPANY.
Good only for One Continuous Passage
LOWVILLE to NEW BREMEN
To be begun on day of sale, as stamped on back hereof by Company's Agent, or before midnight of the following day. In consideration of extended time within which journey may be begun, holder hereof releases Railroad Company from all liability as to baggage for wearing apparel not exceeding in value $100.
Not good if detached from ticket bearing signature.
9231

MANCHESTER & ONEIDA RAILWAY

MANCHESTER & ONEIDA RAILWAY
FROM
MANCHESTER
TO
ONEIDA JUNCTION
GOOD ONLY FOR CONTINUOUS PASSAGE WHEN STAMPED BY COMPANY'S AGENT
A 24326
Form 1   NOT GOOD IF DETACHED
Destination
Via   CHAS PAPER
ISSUED BY

NEW YORK, LAKE ERIE and WESTERN RAILROAD COMPANY
SMITHBORO
TO
BINGHAMTON
Subject to the Company's rules and regulations.
6652

THE NEW YORK, NEW HAVEN & HARTFORD
RAILROAD CO.   603
This Ticket entitles the Bearer to One First-Class Passage to
HOPE VALLEY, R.I.
It is subject to the stop-over regulations of the lines over which it reads
ISSUED BY THE NEW YORK, NEW HAVEN & HARTFORD RAILROAD CO.
WOOD RIVER BRANCH RAILROAD
FIRST CLASS Passage
Wood River Jct. to Hope Valley
Kingston, R.I. to Hope Valley, R.I.
This Check is not good if detached
Gen'l Ticket Agent
603   1941

Disneyland MONORAIL

4 Tickets

Although tickets are the most popular form of railway ephemera, they have never been easy to acquire in genuinely used condition because of the practice in most countries of requiring tickets to be surrendered at the end of the journey. These tickets are sent to a central depot, supposedly kept for a period of time for random checking and then pulped. Seldom has there been any regular system of disposing of used tickets to collectors for security reasons. Even the wholesale closure of lines in the 1950s and 60s yielded relatively few obsolete tickets. Such tickets were often overprinted 'Specimen' or 'Cancelled' to ensure that they could never be reused. As such they are of interest to the specialist, though the average railway enthusiast views them with some disdain. He will generally prefer a ticket which is pocked and scarred with the punches which indicate that it has served its purpose. Over the years collectors have devised many cunning schemes to ensure the retention of their tickets. The most lawful method is that known as overbooking and involves the purchase of a ticket for a destination one stage beyond that actually required. In many cases the railways charged the same price, so little or no extra cost was involved. On alighting at the station one passed through the ticket barrier as if one were quite legitimately breaking the journey, and thus the ticket did not have to be given up. There are other methods – though one should not go as far as a late friend of mine who on at least one occasion impersonated a ticket-collector and relieved the passengers on a train of their tickets!

The evolution of tickets

From the outset the railway companies were greatly troubled by people hitching free rides on their trains and they devised elaborate and complicated schemes to combat this menace. In the early days when trains were still few in number it was possible for the booking-clerk to enter the name of each passenger in his ledger and issue a large paper ticket on which he filled in the name of the agent, the ticket number and the date and time of the train. By the mid-1830s the separate ledger had been replaced by a form of ticket in which the usual details were entered on the right-hand portion which was given to the passenger, while the booking-clerk retained

Opposite Selection of tickets from American railways, including a souvenir ticket for the Nevada Diamond Jubilee celebrations and a ticket for the Disneyland monorail

Right Large paper ticket of the world's premier passenger line, the Stockton and Darlington Railway, England, December 1842

Stockton
TO
Darlington.

NO. *378* Second Class, 1^s 6^d

day of *Dec* 184*2*

Please to hold this Ticket till called for.

Ingenious examples of advertising through the medium of British railway tickets. Note the patent advertising insert, used briefly in the 1930s.

the counterfoil on which was noted the passenger's name, the amount paid and the details of the train. These tickets were often uniface, though an example of the Liverpool to Warrington ticket of 1832 in my collection has a three-line inscription on the back:

NOTICE – No gratuity allowed to be taken by any Guard,
Porter, or other Servant of the Company
Smoking in the First Class Carriages is strictly prohibited.

The second- and third-class carriages being open to the four winds, there was presumably no fear of upsetting non-smokers. These large paper tickets survived for many years and, if anything, tended to get larger and more complex as time went on. The Potteries, Shrewsbury and North Wales Railway continued to use such tickets with matching counterfoils in the 1860s, and despite the invention of the more compact pasteboard ticket, they have survived in certain circumstances to this day.

These paper tickets were not confined to Britain by any means. The United States with its hundreds of independent railroads was forced to resort to tickets of an incredible length – anything up to 5 ft in some cases – which consisted of the basic ticket of the issuing company and a number of checks or coupons bearing the names of the other railroads responsible for various parts of the journey. These checks were perforated so that they could be detached by the conductors *en route*. A train ride from Ajo, Arizona, to Spartanburg, South Carolina, and return, for example, would entail a ticket issued by the Tucson, Cornelia and Gila Bend Railroad with checks bearing the names or initials of the Southern Pacific (Gila Bend to Santa Rosa, New Mexico), Rock Island Line (Santa Rosa to Kansas City), the Chicago, Burlington and Quincy Railroad (Kansas City to Chicago), the New York Central (Chicago to Cincinnati) and the Southern

Left Early paper tickets of the English railways, including an uncut pair of the tickets used by the Liverpool to Warrington Railway in 1832

Railway (Cincinnati to Spartanburg). The return journey by a different route might be just as complicated, involving checks for the Southern (Spartanburg to Atlanta), the Atlanta and West Point Railroad, the Western Railroad of Alabama (West Point to Montgomery), the Louisiana line (Montgomery to New Orleans), the Texas and New Orleans (New Orleans to El Paso), the Southern Pacific (El Paso to Gila Bend) and the Tucson, Cornelia and Gila Bend (Gila Bend to Ajo). A ticket of this type was a valuable document indeed, and the issuing company took the precaution not only of getting the passenger to sign the back of it in the presence of witnesses (who also signed their names) but made provision for the physical description of the passenger, whether male or female, medium, slim or stout, with light, dark or grey hair and of tall, medium or short height – the appropriate descriptions being duly noted with a special ticket-punch.

These highly elaborate tickets were only necessary on long journeys. Curiously enough one could travel right across Europe from London to Constantinople with a much less cumbersome ticket in the form of a booklet with detachable pages similar to a modern airline ticket.

For straightforward journeys involving a single railway company, however, American and Canadian railways usually preferred the small pasteboard ticket. This handy piece of card, one of the unsung blessings of mankind, was invented in 1837 by Thomas Edmondson (1792–1851) who worked as a clerk on the Newcastle and Carlisle Railway. The earliest tickets of this type bore the name of the company, the stations between which they were valid and the class of passenger. The date and the serial number matching the ledger entry were written by hand, though even that process was aided by the invention of the dating press in 1837 and a press for consecutive

Three more examples, including one with pull-out coupon, of advertising through the railway ticket medium

numbering the following year. It was not until the 1850s that all-printed tickets became common. An early practice was to denote the different classes by simple variations in the design. Thus the North British Railway issued tickets inscribed 'First Class & Inside' without any frame-lines, 'Second Class & Outside' with a solid octagonal frame, and 'Third Class & Outside' with a rectangular border of three thin lines. The booking-clerk entered the details of each ticket issued in a ledger and also made out a way-bill for each train on which was written the serial numbers of the tickets opposite columns listing destinations, passengers' names and their class. From the fact that an example of such a way-bill of 1846 in my possession has the actual tickets with it, it may be deduced that at the end of the journey the surrendered tickets were compared with the way-bill (which also travelled on the train) and then filed away together.

The original practice of writing the amount of the fare on the ticket soon lapsed, but in 1890 the railway companies were forced by law to print this on their tickets. By the end of the century tickets usually bore the serial numbers at either end with the date applied at either end on the reverse by means of a dating-machine. The front of the ticket bore the company name, the route, the fare, the class and the type of ticket, and the space on the reverse was often occupied by relevant extracts from the company's regulations.

The actual layout of the inscription varied considerably from company to company and country to country, but the dimensions of 57 mm by 30 mm laid down by Edmondson became standard the world over. Most countries have preferred a horizontal format, though Germany, France, Holland and Switzerland have often used a vertical format, and even some British railway tickets have been produced in this manner.

The tough, unsurfaced pasteboard ticket of the 1840s survived for more than a century and reached its heyday in the years between the two World Wars, both in quality of material and attractiveness of design. Every colour in the spectrum has been used as a background, though the printing is usually in black. Considerable variety could be imparted by using borders, diagonals, vertical stripes, circles and triangles of contrasting colours. Large coloured letters often emphasized the special class of a ticket, and the value might be printed in a more prominent colour.

As a rule the printing on tickets was simple and straightforward with little or no attempt at attractive presentation. From the 1890s, however, many of the American railroads devoted more attention to a pleasing layout and often framed the company name in attractive flourishes. Most Canadian and American tickets were uniface, but in both countries complex background motifs were lithographed before adding the inscriptions in letterpress as a security device, and this greatly enhanced the appearance of the tickets. At the same time the tickets used in North America tended to replace Edmondson's

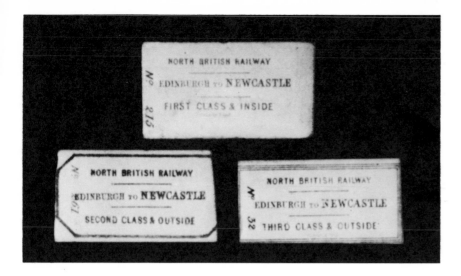

First, second- and third-class tickets of the North British Railway, 1841 – early examples of the Edmondson pasteboard ticket

original stout pasteboard with a thinner card with a more glossy surface, giving them greater visual appeal.

Apart from the security underprints devices for the prevention of fraud include watermarks, and some of the patterns found in the long, composite tickets of America are highly intricate. A watermark was impossible on a pasteboard ticket, so the companies using them experimented with fugitive inks which would run or discolour if anyone tried to erase the date or alter the details in any way. More recently special magnetic inks have been introduced in connection with electronic scanners, used at automatic ticket barriers that dispense with the ticket-collector and his metal punch.

Since 1960 the pasteboard ticket has given way increasingly to much larger tickets in card, semi-card, semi-carton and paper of various types. Many of these tickets are printed at the time of issue and bear coded symbols which are often meaningless to the passenger but greatly simplify the checking processes. Many of them were produced as a result of short-lived experiments and, though largely neglected during their period in use, may well turn out to be the rarities of the future.

Kinds of ticket

Edmondson not only invented the pasteboard ticket, he also produced the world's first ticket rack. Such a device was needed to cope with the multitude of different tickets that any one station might have in stock at any moment. Apart from the tickets bearing the names of all the different destinations and routes from any given place they would have to be kept in duplicate or triplicate, depending on the number of classes, but that was only the beginning. At a very early date the railway companies evolved a complex system of tariffs with special rates for different types of passenger. Half fares or reduced

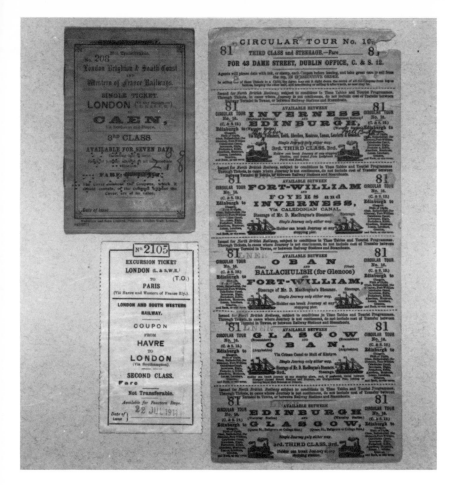

Left Tickets for London to Caen (1883) and London to Paris via Havre (1911), and an elaborate Scottish circular tour ticket of about 1920, involving journeys by steamer and rail. Note the antiquated engravings, reminiscent of 19th-century newspaper advertisements.

rates for children, with or without an adult, resulted in special children's tickets. Excursion rates, special fares on certain days of the week or times of day, were devised to encourage the public to use the railways at off-peak periods. Day returns, three-day returns, period returns and other special tickets are fairly common. Other tickets combined a rail journey with some other mode of transport. Combined tickets may be found with references to coach, bus, motor car, ferryboat and steamship; some complex tourist tickets even have combinations of three or four different transport systems.

Special tickets for the use of clergymen, congressmen and senators, Members of Parliament and deputies have been provided in a number of countries. Bulk users of railways often secure reduced fares, and this is reflected in the special tickets issued to soldiers and sailors, schoolchildren, factory workers and senior citizens. Some of the old British tickets reflect the seasonal nature of agriculture, like the hop-pickers' tickets issued by the Southern Railway or the special tickets for cattle dealers and Irish agricultural labourers. Emigrant tickets issued by the early American railroads are now highly prized, especially those which actually bear the name of the emigrant making

Opposite Thomas Edmondson's patent ticket dating press, designed in conjunction with his pasteboard tickets

his way from New York to the Middle West in the 1870s. World War II is vividly recalled by the many special kinds of ticket then issued by the British companies, including the special three-day excursion tickets that permitted the relatives of evacuees to visit them, the Civil Defence workers' tickets, the distinctive red, white and blue tickets issued to United States Army personnel travelling on duty in London and countless others. One poignant relic is a soldier's travel warrant dated 1 September 1939 – the day Germany invaded Poland and thousands of reservists in Britain and France were mobilized.

Other tickets refer to passenger luggage, dogs, bicycles, mail carts and perambulators, some of which conjure up an interesting picture, such as the London and North-Eastern Railway's ticket for 'One Dog accompanying Passenger from St. Ronan's Clerical Training Centre to any Station not exceeding ten miles distant'. My example has the serial number 63; did 63 would-be clerks at St Ronan's take their pets with them, or did the same dog do the journey 63 times?

Excursion tickets for special events at reduced rates are of additional interest because of the event they commemorate. Tickets may be found referring to Royal Visits, Coronations, Jubilees, Investitures, political rallies and demonstrations, and fairs and exhibitions. In many cases tickets to important exhibitions, like the Toronto Industrial Fair (1897), the Pan-American Exposition (1901), the St Louis World's Fair (1904), the Wembley Exhibition (1924) and the Empire Exhibition in Glasgow (1938), contain references to a particular group of people, and some of these tickets even included the cost of admission to the exhibition itself.

Tickets for special purposes and occasions: (above) ticket issued by London Transport during the Blitz of 1940 permitting people to use the subway as an air raid shelter; Wembley Exhibition, 1924; King's Cross Centenary, 1952; (right) country auction; Welch miner's; Royal visit to Edinburgh; Irish agricultural labourer's; World War I combined leave and rail ticket from the Western Front; bicycle; cattle dealer's; Empire Exhibition excursion, 1938; perambulator

Before World War I there were special tickets for concert parties and theatrical touring companies, often bearing the names of impresarios and actor-managers whose names have since become part of theatre and vaudeville history.

Season tickets and commutation tickets (from which we get the ugly modern word 'commuter') form an interesting group, varying from a ten-ride weekly to quarterly and even annual tickets. Some enterprising companies even offered an eternal ticket, sumptuously printed and mounted in gold-blocked leather. I wonder how many people who had the foresight to beat inflation in this manner still have these relics of a bygone age.

Platform tickets form a very large group in themselves, enabling people to meet their friends off a train on the actual platform without the problem of having a rail ticket. The earliest platform tickets were made of black-enamelled brass with serial numbers engraved on them and an inscription indicating that they had to be surrendered on leaving the platform. Later, pasteboard and then carton tickets were substituted. Their purpose is usually self-explanatory and, of course, they differ from train tickets by having only the name of the station or depot on them. Many of them were valid for one hour only, and this was indicated by holes punched through the hour number.

Generally speaking a small charge was made for these platform tickets, but a curious exception was the ticket issued free by the Great Western Railway 'for the sole purpose of permitting the holder to proceed to the UP Booking Office at Taunton Station via the Company's platforms and subway to purchase a ticket for a railway journey'. London Transport even had shelter tickets, grimly evocative of the Blitz, with the inscription 'Persons permitted to use this Station as . . . an Air Raid Shelter do so at their own risk in all respects'.

Relatively few tickets have had a pictorial motif on them. Some of the suburban railroads of America have had tickets with a picture of the railcar as part of the underprint, and a similar device may

Platform tickets from Britain and Australia, including the ticket issued at Llanfairpwllgwyngyllgogerychwyrn-drobwllllantysiliogogogoch, possibly the station with the longest name in the world

Above Free passes in ivory or bronze, including an example named to a specific individual

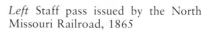

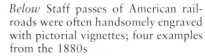

Left Staff pass issued by the North Missouri Railroad, 1865

Below Staff passes of American railroads were often handsomely engraved with pictorial vignettes; four examples from the 1880s

be found on some European tickets. Others feature famous landmarks and tourist attractions and make attractive souvenirs of foreign travel. Suburban and inter-urban lines in several European countries, notably Germany, Hungary and Italy, have had large paper tickets which incorporate maps and diagrams of the routes – a curious aspect of cartography which is usually overlooked by map collectors.

The rarest form of ticket is the railway pass and these were often highly decorative. The most desirable of all were the passes, in gold, silver or ivory, which were presented to promoters and directors of the old railway companies, often guaranteeing them free travel over the company lines for life. More mundane, but very elusive, are the staff passes used by the railmen (and sometimes their families) in bronze, brass, pewter or white metal. Large ornate complimentary tickets and passes were produced in connection with many of the ceremonies that celebrated the opening or extension of a line. They were handsomely engraved and often bore tiny vignettes of scenery and locomotives. Their modern counterpart is the souvenir ticket produced by several of the railway museums, but that is a poor substitute for what can justly be regarded as the very acme of the railway ticket as an art form.

Opposite Assorted ephemera of British, North American, Australian and Rhodesian railways, including a Forces' leave ticket, a season ticket, a school pupil ticket, a dog ticket, free passes and official stationery

5 Timetables and guides

The railways have spawned a remarkable volume of literature, but nothing gladdens the heart of the collector so much as the early timetables and guides published by the railway companies and other interested parties.

The earliest trains hardly knew the meaning of the word time, their time of departure was imponderable and their arrival a downright uncertainty. The advertising of train departures was tentative at best and took the form of brief newspaper announcements and handbills for each individual train. Timetables continued to be no more than a leaflet printed on both sides until the mid-1830s, reciting the modest routes and listing the stations and termini. They gave the tables of fares and parcel rates, but when it came to naming actual times they tended to be rather vague. The pioneer timetables often included references to connections with steam packets and mail coaches. The most interesting of all are those which showed that only certain trains were hauled by locomotive engines and others were still relying on horse traction.

The tremendous growth of the railways in the premier decade inspired Bradshaw of London to publish a timetable in book form, listing all the services in Britain. The first edition of Bradshaw's *Railway Time Table and Assistant to Railway Travelling* was a tiny, slim volume issued in 1839 and sold for one shilling. It gave the times of trains, the fares charged and useful hints to the would-be traveller unused to this new mode of transport. The most interesting feature, however, was the series of hand-coloured maps of the routes then in existence, together with lines in progress of construction and others which had been proposed. Town plans and vignettes of interesting landmarks added to the value of 'Bradshaw', as this commercial guide soon became known.

Bradshaws were published for more than a century and waxed and waned as did the railways whose timetables they contained. In their heyday they were hefty tomes which required no small skill and patience to read correctly and often confused and exasperated their users. As happens so often with other national institutions they were often abused and criticized, but the railway world is a sadder place for their passing. Significantly, various editions of vintage Bradshaws have been reprinted in recent years.

Front cover of a pictorial fold-out timetable and route map of the Lake Shore and Michigan Southern Railway, 1882

Opposite Pictorial testimonial presented by the Association of Locomotive Engineers and Firemen (ASLEF) to their Branch Chairman, Sir A. Morley; British, 1925

Above Timetable for the Lake Shore and Michigan Southern Railway, 1882

Below Cover of the first edition of Bradshaw's *Railway Companion*, published in London at a shilling in 1838

The railway companies produced their own timetables, and these are often of great interest on account of the way in which the individual companies advertised their best features to the travelling public. The finest timetables were those produced at the turn of the century. They were often cloth-bound with gold blocked illustrations on the cover and were profusely illustrated inside. Eventually they combined the function of a timetable with that of a tourist guide, and this element continues to the present day. After World War I these timetable-guides adopted eye-catching paper covers which often highlighted the more glamorous lines and express trains. This reached its peak in America in the 30s but was copied elsewhere to a lesser degree.

Since World War II timetables have become more prosaic again. Nationalization and amalgamations have reduced the number of competing companies and the need for the publicity element. The major timetables published by Amtrak, Canadian National Railways, British Rail, New Zealand Railways, SNCF in France and the German *Bundesbahn* are strictly factual tomes; but at the same time most railways still indulge in smaller timetables covering a single route or region, and often these brochures are attractively illustrated with ancillary matter aimed at the tourist trade.

Apart from the timetables for the benefit of the public every railway line has its working timetables, staff manuals and rule books. At the time of their currency these publications were restricted to company personnel and were closely guarded but over the years many of them have come into the hands of collectors and students of railway history. The tables are usually much more detailed than those found in passenger timetables and contain copious notes on signals, the use of pilot engines, goods trains, the use of sidings and even the inspection and collection of tickets. Old rule books and manuals gave detailed instructions on everything from accidents, announcements and automatic machines to wagons, weighing-machines and Westinghouse brake-systems. Every station-master, inspector, engine-driver, fireman, guard, signalman, policeman, ganger, foreman, shunter, yardman, gatekeeper, clerk and porter was given a copy of the company rule book and expected to carry it with him for production on demand. He was also expected to know it backward and would frequently be catechized on its contents. There were special working timetables and manuals for such services as the travelling or railway post offices. Some of these timetables were so detailed that they even contained route maps and diagrams showing every bridge and crossing, every river, junction and platform *en route* with the precise times at which these features were to be passed.

Bradshaw was not the only publisher of timetables giving data on more than one company simultaneously. The *ABC* and Murray's guides concentrated on the companies operating in a specific region, and there were quite tiny timetables, produced by many printers and

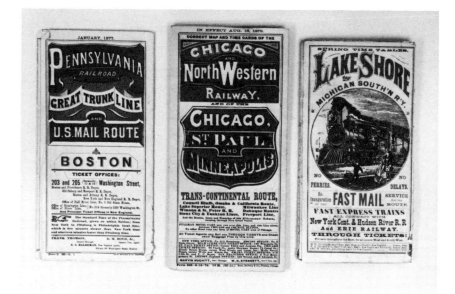

stationers, which were sold for a penny and gave the details of train services in a limited area, perhaps to and from a single town. These unofficial timetables are just as collectable as the company publications and often more informative because they were impartial. Similar timetables were produced in America and Europe, and one of their interesting features was the large amount of commercial, non-railway advertising which they carried, giving a valuable insight into life in the late nineteenth and early twentieth centuries.

Allied to the timetables were the itineraries published by some railway companies but more usually of private origin. These took the form of a concertina strip of paper which opened out to show a map of the route with prominent landmarks and points of interest featured. From time to time such itineraries are produced to this day and they are worth looking for.

The railways also published guidebooks which had little or no direct reference to the running of their trains but were intended to interest tourists and would-be travellers. Again, the heyday of this form of promotional literature was between the two World Wars.

Of an earlier vintage altogether was the religious material purveyed by some railway companies. This arose primarily in the 1840s when the first trains were allowed to run on Sundays. At least one American state, Vermont, passed a law requiring the conductor on Sunday trains to read passages of the Scriptures to his passengers and provided special bibles for the purpose. Station waiting-rooms in England in the 1870s and 80s had their *Hand-book of Inspired Thought about God and His People selected from the Psalms,* the forerunner of the modern Gideon Bible, to minister to the spiritual needs of the traveller.

Above Pictorial broadsheet advertising the Boston and Lowell Railroad's excursion to Lake Winnipesaukee, 1884. The railway companies were quick to assess the potential of tourism in boosting traffic.

Right Travelling chart published by the Railway Chronicle for the London–Dover route, 1892

Above Handbill advertising cheap excursions on the Glasgow and South-Western Railway, 1887

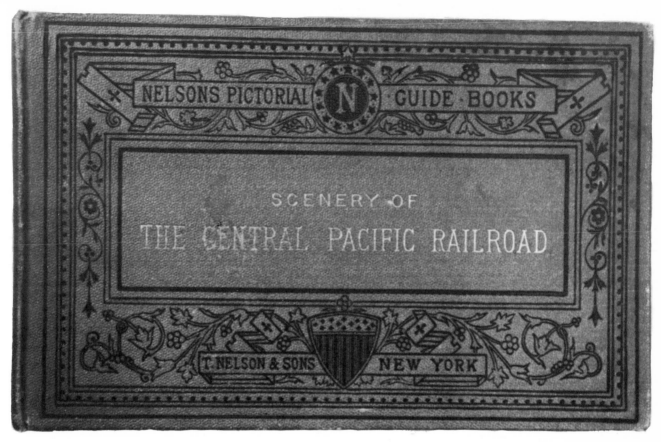

Above One of the popular series of Nelson's Pictorial Guide Books, *Scenery of the Central Pacific Railroad* was published shortly after the completion of the line in 1869.

Right Leaflet advertising the tariff for meals and apartments at the Caledonian Railway's Central Station Hotel, Glasgow, *c.* 1890

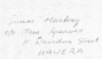

6 Railway philately

For many years there has been a rumour, so far unsubstantiated by documentary evidence, that a Scottish horse-drawn mineral railway introduced adhesive labels to denote the prepayment of freight charges on parcels carried on its wagons. The year of this alleged service was 1811, and should actual specimens of these stamps turn up, they would antedate the world's recognized first stamps, the Penny Black and Twopenny Blue, by some twenty-nine years.

Mail-bags were carried on the trains of the Liverpool and Manchester Railway almost from its inception in 1830 but only on an unofficial basis. The first railway mail in the United States was carried by the *Best Friend* on the South Carolina Railroad in January 1831 but likewise on an unofficial basis. The annual report of the American Postmaster General in 1834 made the first official mention of the carriage of mail by railroad, but this was no more than a recommendation, and a further four years elapsed before the first mail contract was negotiated between the USPO and the railroads, following an Act of Congress on 7 July 1838. The first mail contract of this kind, however, was arranged in Britain some months earlier when George Louis, Superintendent of Mail Coaches, organized a connection between the London–Birmingham stage-coach and the trains of the Grand Junction Railway running from Birmingham to Liverpool. Special carriages, manned by post-office clerks who sorted the mail picked up *en route,* were designed and put into service in January 1838. Ingenious apparatus for picking up and putting down mailbags from trains running at full speed were devised by Nathaniel Worsdell and John Ramsay and were introduced in March 1839.

The system was originally known as the Railway Post Office or RPO – a term which was soon discontinued in Britain though it was used until recently in America. The term Travelling Post Office (TPO) was adopted instead and appears in the special postmarks applied to mail sorted and stamped *en route*. Many of the old-time postmarks bore the initails SC (Sorting Carriage) or ST (Sorting Tender). Other clues to the identity of railway postmarks are such words as 'Night Down', 'Up Special', 'Day Up' or the grouping of two or more names of towns, indicating the termini of the route.

The Railway Post Office was not established in the United States until March 1865, though there had been a number of experiments in

Early examples of locomotives featured on postage stamps. The stamp of Transvaal (centre left) was the first commemorative stamp in Africa (1895)

Opposite Railway covers and philatelic items: souvenir of New Zealand's 'Kingston Flyer' with vignette, stamp and postmark to match; stationery of the Manchester, Sheffield and Lincolnshire Railway, 1879; memento of the Talyllyn Railway with private rail stamp; pictorial cover and postmark of the Vale of Rheidol Railway; cover from the Royal Train during the visit of King George VI and Queen Elizabeth to Canada, 1939; maximum card showing a railway sorting carriage, with matching stamp

mail-sorting in trains over a period of several years. President Van Buren had first sanctioned the use of the railroads in 1838, and seven years later mail facilities were provided on certain lines. The first experimental mail car was introduced on the Hannibal and St Joseph Railroad in 1862, and the Chicago and Northwestern Railway anticipated the 1865 Act of Congress by running a Railway Post Office in August 1864. American postmarks bore the initials RPO (Railway Post Office) or RMS (Railway Mail Service) and eventually denoted the termini, the name of the line or the name of the train as well.

Railways were established in Canada from 1836 onwards, but it was not until 1851, when the Canadian Post Office was reorganized, that provision was made for the establishment of the Railway Post Office. Distinctive postmarks were introduced in 1853 for the St Lawrence and Atlantic and the Ontario, Simcoe and Huron Railroads. The early postmarks bore the names of the railway, and distinctive date-stamps were allocated to each conductor and mail clerk. The later postmarks bore the names or initials of the termini and letters such as R or RW to denote the railway.

Similar services were eventually adopted by every other country, and the collecting of envelopes and postcards bearing the distinctive railway postmarks is now a major branch of philately. European postmarks may be recognized by the letters AMB – an abbreviation for *Ambulant* or *Ambulancia* – or the German words *Zug* (train) or *Bahnpost* (railway post). Some philatelists also include marks inscribed *Banen*, *Bahn*, *Ferrovia*, *Gare* or *Station*, indicating mail posted at a railway station though not necessarily carried by rail.

Railway stamps

If we except the apocryphal tale of 1811, the earliest adhesive labels denoting the prepayment of freight charges on parcels carried by rail date from 1855 when the various companies in Britain began using them. A parcel service operated by the General Post Office did not appear until 1883 and even thereafter it did not have a monopoly of parcel traffic. Consequently the railway companies, together with road haulage contractors, bus companies and private carriers, continued to issue their own labels for this purpose. The early labels were often beautifully engraved with the company's insignia and sometimes tiny vignettes of trains, ships and parcel vans. Labels were produced for a variety of purposes ranging from the all-purpose label simply inscribed 'Parcel' to those inscribed 'Newspapers', 'Milk-churn', 'Farm Produce', 'Samples' or 'Market Basket'. From 1900 onwards they became more functional in appearance and dwindled in number as companies amalgamated, were regrouped and finally nationalized. Distinctive parcel labels were used by the railways in many countries, some of the most attractive being those which the

Australian state railways use to this day. In some countries, such as Belgium and Bulgaria, where the carriage of parcels was a state monopoly in the hands of the railways, special railway stamps are issued under the authority of the post office, and many attractive designs have been produced down to the present day.

The carriage of letters, as distinct from parcels, is a monopoly which has been jealously guarded by the state for many years. Apart from the advantages accruing from carriage and sorting on the RPOs and TPOs it was found expedient to introduce a special railway express service whereby letters could be carried on trains under special circumstances. Thus a letter could be handed in at a station for transmission by train to its destination and either called for at the terminus or posted in the normal way. In 1891 the British Postmaster General relaxed the regulations and permitted the railway companies to accept letters in this way, provided that these letters bore a penny stamp for the postage and a special twopenny stamp to cover the rail fee. Special railway letter stamps in more or less uniform designs but with the individual company names were introduced in that year and survived until the 1920s. Thereafter they were gradually superseded by parcel stamps or hand-struck marks inscribed 'Railway Express' or 'Railex'. They have been revived in recent years by some of the private light railways and lines operated by preservation societies. While these modern examples seldom serve any real purpose and are philatelically inspired, they make a very attractive addition to any collection of railwayana.

Many of the railway companies had their own stamped stationery or distinctive envelopes, wrappers and cards for use on company business. Letters endorsed or stamped OCS (On Company Service) or RRS (Railroad Service) are highly prized by philatelists. The more elaborate envelopes bore impressions of 'stamps' similar to the adhesive labels and were widely used at one time by newspaper correspondents, coal agents and other individuals who needed to

Above Stamps used in connection with railway letter or parcel services. Bavarian postage stamp (centre left) overprinted 'E' denoted use on the railways (*Eisenbahn*)

send urgent communications by rail. One should not overlook ordinary government postage stamps perforated with the initials of the railway companies as a security precaution. These stamps, properly used and still affixed to envelopes bearing the printed endorsement and embossed seals of the old companies, are much sought after.

Philately with a railway theme

Many postage stamps not specifically provided for railway mail depict a locomotive and are thus of great interest to philatelists and railway buffs alike. The earliest postage stamp to depict a locomotive was issued by a private mail delivery company, the Broadway Post Office of New York, in 1848 – anticpating by twenty-one years the three-cents stamp of the USPO featuring a wood-burning locomotive of the late 1860s. The first government-issued stamp to picture a locomotive was issued by the Canadian province of New Brunswick in May 1860, and some controversy centres on this stamp. It was thought that the stamp showed the locomotive *Ossekeag*, Number 9, of the European and North American Railway which was opened in 1857 between Pointe du Chêne and Moncton, a distance of nineteen miles. In August 1860 the line was extended from Saint John to Shediac, a distance of 108 miles, and the one-cent stamp was regarded as a somewhat premature celebration of this event. Closer examination of the design, however, reveals that the locomotive more closely resembles one used on the Atlantic and St Lawrence Railway, but the truth is that the picture is a combination of both types. The engraver employed by the American Bank Note Company of New York probably used artistic licence in evolving the design.

Railway philately: commemorative stamps from Europe and Africa showing rolling-stock old and new

Two years after the three-cents stamp of the United States was introduced, Peru issued a curious embossed stamp showing a locomotive. This stamp of 1871 celebrated the twentieth anniversary of the opening of the line between Lima, Callao and Chorillos and is now regarded as the world's first ever commemorative stamp. No other stamps in this theme appeared until 1895 when Uruguay issued a pictorial series with a locomotive on the five centesimos and Mexico featured a train on the peso denominations of a new definitive set. In the same year the South African Republic (Transvaal) celebrated the introduction of penny postage with a large-sized stamp showing mail communications old and new – a stage-coach and a mail train. Several Latin American countries, including El Salvador, Honduras and Ecuador, had stamps with a railway motif at the turn of the century, while the two-cents stamp in the Pan-American Exposition series of 1901 showed a modern express train. Mail trains were featured on the American parcel post five cents of 1912, a Belgian railway parcels series of 1916 and also on a Russian famine relief semi-postal of 1922.

Commemorative stamps still being in their infancy in the 20s, Britain let slip the opportunity to issue railway commemoratives in either 1925 or 1930. Even the United States belatedly honoured the Baltimore and Ohio Railroad in 1952 with a stamp marking its 125th anniversary. It was left to Germany (1935), Italy and the Netherlands (both 1939) to commemorate railway centenaries with special stamps.

Since then centennial issues have become an ever-increasing feature of railway philately and even lesser anniversaries have been honoured. Thus the seventy-fifth anniversary of the completion of the Transcontinental Railroad was celebrated by a three-cents stamp of 1944 showing the Golden Spike ceremony. Six years later the fiftieth anniversary of the death of Casey Jones on 30 April 1900 was marked by a three-cents stamp bearing his portrait and honouring Railroad Engineers of America. France has issued stamps for the centenary of the *Ambulant* service of 1844, while one of Bulgaria's mourning stamps for the late King Boris III showed him in his favourite role on the footplate of the Orient Express.

In recent years there have been hundreds of stamps depicting locomotives old and new. Even Britain, who started the whole thing off, eventually got around to a set in 1975 marking the 150th anniversary of the Stockton and Darlington Railway. Slogan postmarks, commemorative handstamps, souvenir envelopes and cards and presentation packs and booklets add considerably to the interest and variety of railway philately.

Above Railway philately: stamps commemorating railway anniversaries from Jamaica, Canada, Australia and America, the latter honouring Casey Jones

Below (left) Official pictorial envelope of 1890 celebrating the Golden Jubilee of British Penny Postage; (right) the caricature by Harry Furniss transforming the North Mail train into 'The Post Office profit, 1890, swallowed up by the million'

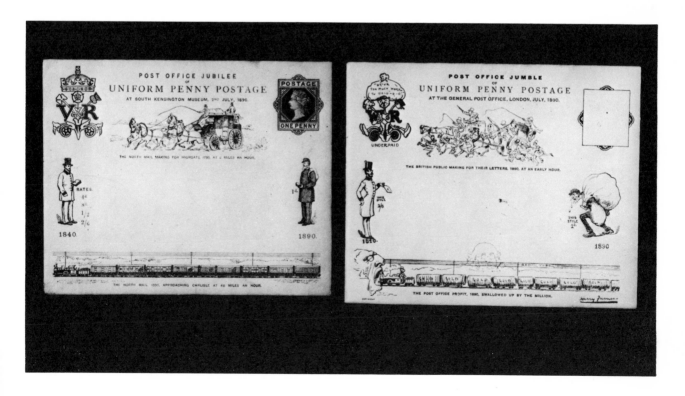

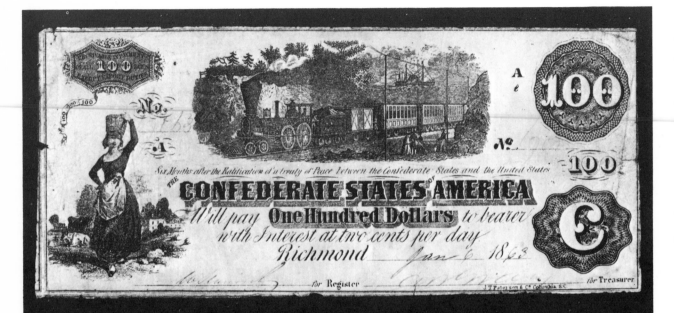

7 Railway numismatics

A little-known feature of the early American railroads was that their charter of incorporation often included banking privileges. They were authorized by Congress to issue their own paper money, and many thousands of dollars' worth of these handsome notes were printed in the period from about 1850 to the middle 1880s when the privilege was rescinded. Few of these companies took the opportunity of depicting actual locomotives or scenes relevant to their lines. The majority of the notes were produced by security printers in New York and Philadelphia, and the choice of subject was usually left to their engravers. Nevertheless, the railroad currency which played a vital part in the development of the West is of interest to railway collectors and social historians alike.

Government notes also featured early locomotives, one of the most highly prized nowadays being the $100 bill issued by the Confederate States of America at Richmond in 1862–3. The principal motif was a train of the Civil War period, complete with carriages, freight-wagon tender and locomotive, the last-named having a cowcatcher and a disproportionately large smoke-stack. The Latin American countries, such as Mexico and Guatemala, and the prolific Chinese banks of the 1920s issued many banknotes featuring locomotives. More than anything else the railway signified civilization and modernity, particularly in countries which were still relatively underdeveloped.

Trains and locomotives were a popular feature also on the notes issued by many of the small town and country banks which flourished briefly (and often crashed spectacularly) in Britain and America a century ago. Curiously enough this was not a subject which ever made much impact on European banknotes, though locomotives were inevitably featured on some of the myriads of emergency notes (*Notgeld*) produced in Germany and Austria during the inflation of 1923, and a locomotive of the Trans-Siberian Railway appeared on Russian banknotes. Turkish notes featured a railway cutting, and Yugoslav notes showed locomotive wheels.

Coins and tokens

Regrettably the railways have made even less of an impact on the coins of the world, only three countries having so far given it

Opposite (top) obverse of the $100 bill issued by the Confederate States of America, depicting a steamship and a wood-burning locomotive of the 1860s; (bottom) the Trans-Siberian Railway featured on the 50-kopek note of the Russian Asiatic Bank, *c.* 1910

prominence. The first coin ever to mention railways was the silver milreis of Brazil, one of a set of four released in 1900 to celebrate the quatercentenary of the discovery of Brazil. The Liberty head on the obverse was surrounded by tiny motifs symbolizing progress, and a railway was one of the symbols chosen. The quatercentenary of colonization was celebrated in 1932 by a set of six coins, one of which showed a nineteenth-century locomotive on the reverse, while the obverse portrayed Viscount de Maua (1813–89), builder of the first line from Rio de Janeiro to Petropolis in 1856. The opening of the Southern Railway linking Yucatán and Mexico City was commemorated by Mexico in 1950 with a silver five-peso coin showing a locomotive, palm trees and the rising sun on the obverse.

A line of a totally different kind was the subject of a commemorative twenty-five-pence coin issued by the Isle of Man in 1976. This coin celebrated the centenary of the island's distinctive horse-drawn trams and featured a streetcar of a type which has been in continuous use since the beginning of this century. Incidentally, the island runs one of the last state-owned steam lines anywhere in Europe, as well as an electric railway and a mountain railway to the summit of Snaefell – all of which have been the subject of special stamps and postmarks in recent years.

Tokens of various kinds have been provided by or for the railways at different times. A relic of the construction gangs, the navvies and gandy dancers of the nineteenth century, is the array of tokens in pewter, brass, bronze and white metal, which were used to pay the men. These tokens could only be exchanged for goods at the company store – a subtle form of exploitation which was banned by the Anti-Truck Acts but persisted none the less. The token system was used in many parts of the world – from Canada to Uganda, from America to the farthest shores of Asia. Most of these tokens were purely functional in appearance with little more than the initials of the company and the nominal value cast or struck on one side. However, very few tokens were struck on both sides or bore a company crest.

More sophisticated in appearance were the tokens used by railway employees, public servants and certain other groups to travel by train without the need for an actual cash transaction. These tokens were issued by many of the railway and tramway companies and had a specific cash value so that they could be exchanged when required for a ticket of the desired amount. The earlier tokens were struck in bronze or brass, though some are known in pewter, white metal, zinc and aluminium, and more recent examples have been recorded in plastic. The more attractive examples depicted locomotives and rolling-stock, though usually the company name and coat of arms sufficed. Similar tokens were issued by local authorities for use by public employees and can be distinguished by their inscription and emblems relating to the town or municipality.

French tramway and railway token, 1904

Railway medals

The Victorians struck medals to commemorate all manner of events, both national and parochial, and inevitably the coming of the railways was duly recorded in this fashion. Medals were struck to mark the opening of the Liverpool and Manchester Railway in 1830 and the Grand Junction Railway seven years later. Thereafter every new line opened and every company launched was accompanied by one or more medals. Apart from the locomotives (which were not depicted as often as one might expect) these medals featured the company crest and, more often than not, a picture of a viaduct or similar feat of engineering, or the imposing façade of the principal station on the line.

The fashion for medals waned at the end of the nineteenth century but revived in the 1930s at a time when many important centenaries were being celebrated. Medals of this period include those featuring the *Rocket* for the centenary of the Liverpool and Manchester Railway (1930) and the 150th anniversary of the birth of George Stephenson the following year. Other relatively modern medals marked the passage of the Railways Act of 1921 which led to the regrouping of the British companies into four major lines, the breaking of the world record for steam traction and the withdrawal of the last steam trains in the 1960s. The 150th anniversary of the Stockton and Darlington Railway in 1975 triggered off a spate of medals in gold and silver as well as base metals, and doubtless other sesquicentennials on both sides of the Atlantic will be celebrated in this way in years to come. In Canada and the United States the scope of these commemoratives is much greater than in Britain since many of the building contractors and engineering companies supplying parts and equipment have also struck medals commemorating the railways. Furthermore, the survival of many of the old companies into the 1950s enabled many of them to strike medals honouring their centenaries. Medals were also struck in the interwar period to publicize the lines, to promote safety, in connection with exhibitions or merely for propaganda purposes.

Many railway companies produced long-service medals which they awarded to their veteran employees. First-aid and safety competitions were held annually and the winners received appropriate medals. The most coveted of all, however, are the gallantry medals awarded by the British railway companies and the London Passenger Transport Board in recognition of the fact that railway workers were just as much in the front line during the Blitz as any combat troops. These medals were awarded for individual acts of heroism. Only nine Bravery Medals were awarded by the London Passenger Transport Board, and such was their high standing that the recipients were also automatically awarded the George Medal – Britain's second highest award to civilians. These railway medals of World War II must surely rank among the rarest gallantry awards ever made.

Above Medal of the Institution of Locomotive Engineers, depicting Stephenson's *Rocket*

Below Bravery medal awarded by the Lancashire and Yorkshire Railway to James Clarkson, 5 July 1861

8 Ephemera

Mention has already been made of the vast amount of paperwork which running a railway entailed. Modern computerized processes have drastically reduced the oceans of forms, vouchers, cards and way-bills which at one time accompanied every action of the railway, from the dispatch of a single parcel or passenger to an entire goods train. Much of this paperwork was filed away in individual depots and stations or consigned to attics and vaults in the company headquarters to moulder away quietly over the years. Salvage drives during World War II liberated a great deal, but the closure of the unecomonic lines in the postwar years brought much more of this material to light. Even now the occasional chest or cupboard full of papers is unearthed from time to time, but instead of being consigned to the scrap-merchant it is eagerly pounced on by collectors.

One can learn a lot not only about the running of old railways but also about the mode of life and the commerce of a town or district in days gone by from a perusal of these forms. The railways had a regular system of daily, weekly, monthly and quarterly returns to head office of the passenger traffic and freight they handled, and one can soon get some idea of the importance of the railway in any community from these documents. The Great North of Scotland Railway Company, for example, had a large monthly sheet itemizing the freight handled. Live Stock was one general heading, sub-divided into Horses, Donkeys and Ponies, Cattle, Calves, Sheep and Lambs, Pigs and Other Animals. Then there was 'General Goods', followed by such items of individual importance as Whisky, Fish, Timber, Agricultural Produce, Manure, Coal, Lime and Stones – giving us a clear idea of the exports of the remoter Highland districts at the turn of the century. Other forms one may encounter include Parcel Delivery sheets, Consignment Notes for Perishable Goods sent at Owner's Risk, Coal-merchants forms, Counterfoils and Way-bills. The last-named can be divided into those dealing with passenger traffic itemizing each ticket issued, as mentioned in Chapter 4, or dealing with freight. There were special way-bills for 'Horses, Cattle, Dogs and other Quadrupeds', Poultry and other Live Birds, Carriages, Bicycles, Tricycles, Perambulators, Bath Chairs, Excess Luggage and even Corpses. These way-bills were filled out by the consigning station and given to the guard or conductor of the train,

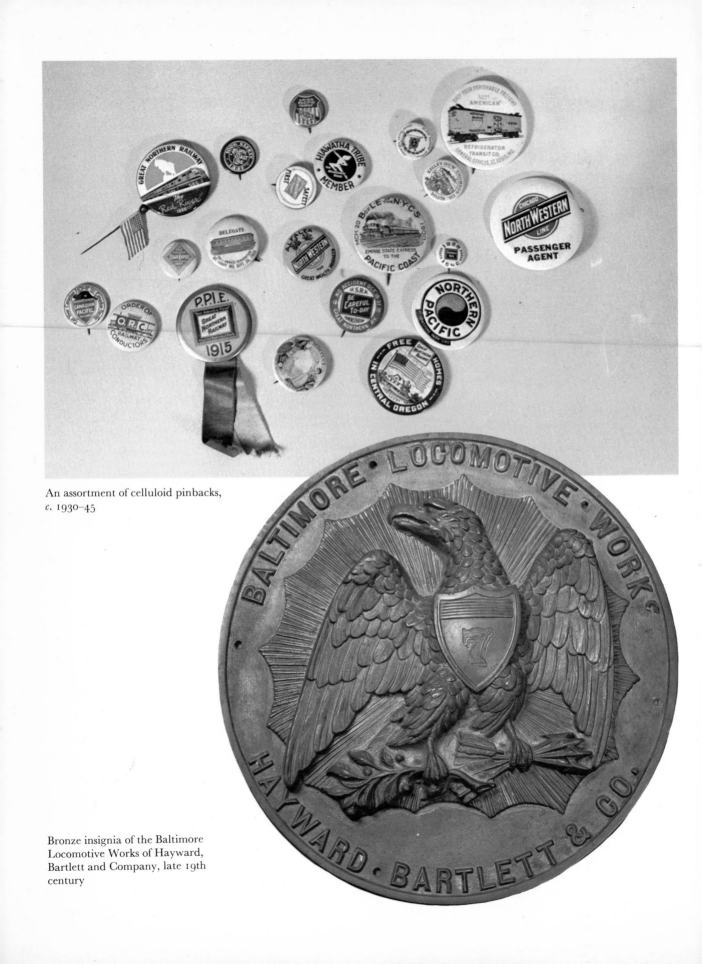

An assortment of celluloid pinbacks,
c. 1930–45

Bronze insignia of the Baltimore
Locomotive Works of Hayward,
Bartlett and Company, late 19th
century

who delivered it to the officer on duty at the receiving station or depot. Each company differed in the items listed on these way-bills or the amount of detail given, though few went as far as the Great Eastern Railway in distinguishing the sex of the animals it transported.

The railway companies had their own distinctive headed notepaper and envelopes, and these are quite collectable. The earliest lines had elegant notepaper with a relatively plain copperplate heading, but by the turn of the century the more progressive companies, especially in Canada and the United States, had lithographed or engraved vignettes covering the top of the sheet and often extending down the left-hand side as well. Stationery alluding to the railways was also used by haulage contractors, coal-merchants and hotels, reflecting their dependence on the railway for so much of their business. From 1870 onwards postcards were also employed, and many of them will be found with printed text on the reverse relating to the transportation of freight.

By the beginning of this century the more enterprising companies were providing pictorial notepaper, envelopes and cards for the use of passengers, often featuring scenery on the major routes, pictures of trains and spaces for the writer to insert the date and the route.

When the picture postcard craze was at its height in the early years of this century, many railways published sets of cards depicting

Grand Trunk Railway Christmas card, 1898

locomotives and rolling-stock, old and new, the scenic attractions of their lines and even views of stations, depots and railway hotels. Many cards show bridges and viaducts, junctions and even prosaic scenes of sidings and goods yards. Individual cards, especially those with a TPO or RPO postmark for good measure, are worth looking for, but unused cards, long neglected by collectors primarily interested in stamps and postmarks, have now returned to fashion and are much in demand. Many of these cards were published in sets, and complete series still in their original packets (themselves highly decorative) are keenly sought after. The Canadian Pacific Railway even designed the packet itself in such a way that the entire series could be transmitted through the post inside it and provided spaces for the stamp and the address on the front. Many of the scenic cards published in Britain were produced by the railways whose crest appears discreetly in a corner of the picture or tucked away on the reverse side. These crested cards are also much in demand nowadays. Then there are the countless postcards of private manufacture which feature railway stations, bridges and locomotives, and these are also eminently collectable since they help to dress up a collection of railwayana associated with a particular area. In recent years museums and preservation societies have published their own postcards featuring vintage locomotives, rolling-stock and railway antiques.

Above and opposite far right Group of picture postcards, 1900–25, including scenic cards bearing company crests, published by railways to promote tourism on their routes

Right Series of picture postcards portraying railway employees, published by the Canadian Pacific Railway, *c.* 1930

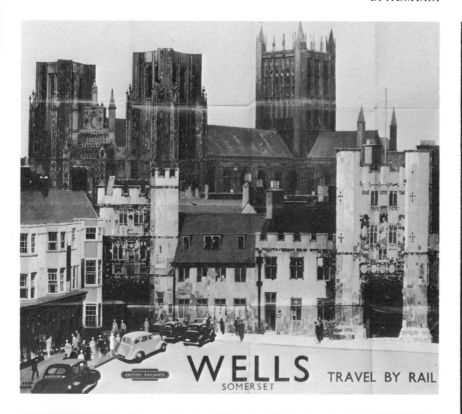

Above left British Railways poster advertising Wells, Somerset, *c.* 1952

Left Compagnie Internationale des Wagons-Lits poster advertising the weekly Constantza Express linking Ostend and Constantinople, 1901

Right Pictorial cards showing railway scenery, from two packs issued by the Intercolonial and Grand Trunk Railway of Canada, 1910

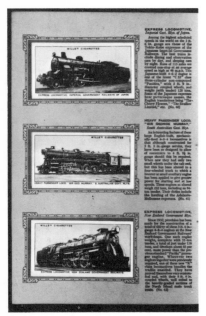

Three cigarette cards from a series published about 1930 by W. D. and H. O. Wills of England featuring famous express locomotives of Japan, Australia and New Zealand. The matching album was sold through tobacconists for a penny

Although today there is much less competition between different companies, there is still a vast amount of advertising matter, all of which is potentially collectable. The heyday of this promotional material, however, was the period between the World Wars when rival companies vied with each other in producing eye-catching posters, handbills and leaflets advertising the tourist attractions served by their lines. The earliest posters had wood-block engravings and a variety of mixed founts of type which have a strange period flavour nowadays. Chromolithography raised the railway poster to the status of an art form in the 1890s. Some of the elegant picture posters of that period have now been reprinted but can easily be distinguished from the originals which are exceedingly elusive. Many railway companies also published prints featuring paintings of their locomotives, and these look most attractive when mounted and framed.

The railways lost no opportunity of promoting themselves in many other kinds of paper ephemera. Book-markers decorated with pictures of trains and maps of the route were popular at the turn of the century. Some companies, particularly in America, even went so far as publishing packs of playing cards whose backs were decorated with pictures of locomotives. Matchbooks, invented in the United States in the 1890s, swiftly became the most popular form of advertising used by the railroads and many are produced to this day. The idea of the matchbook has never caught on in Britain to any great extent, but everywhere else one will find examples of these handy match dispensers bearing advertisements and pictures of the world's railways. One of the most attractive is the series produced by New Zealand Railways depicting veteran locomotives from the Age

of Steam. The back of these matchbooks, of course, advertises the modern expresses operated by NZR.

So far as I am aware no railway has ever produced its own brand of cigarettes or cigars, but many of the tobacco companies used railway motifs to decorate cigarette packets and cigar boxes, and a popular subject in the cigarette cards before World War II was locomotives. These cards, originally intended as stiffeners in the early paper packs, were pioneered in the United States in the 1870s but they died out in the country of origin at the turn of the century when the American Tobacco Company forced its competitors out of business. In Britain, however, the situation was reversed when the American Tobacco Company waged war with the companies in that country and both sides used cigarette cards in a bid to attract the smoking public. Even after the battle was resolved by the formation of the two giant combines, the British American Tobacco Company and the Imperial Tobacco Company, the war of the cigarette cards continued until wartime shortages of material led to their demise in 1940.

Many of the British companies and their subsidiaries in Australia and New Zealand issued sets of cards featuring famous railway engines, trains and railway working. Some companies, notably Churchman and Wills, issued several sets, each consisting of fifty cards. Ogden and Hignett Brothers both had similar sets of modern railways (in the 1920s), while R. and J. Hill produced sets in both standard and large sizes to celebrate the railway centenary in 1925. R. J. Lea did a series of seventy transfers featuring world locomotives in 1926, and Pattreioeux even published a set of cigarette cards reproducing railway posters by famous artists. W. D. & H. O. Wills produced several sets entitled Railway Engines or Railway Loco-

Compagnie Internationale des Wagons-Lits menu for 6 December 1884. Note the pictorial decoration showing the Company's dining-car in the centre

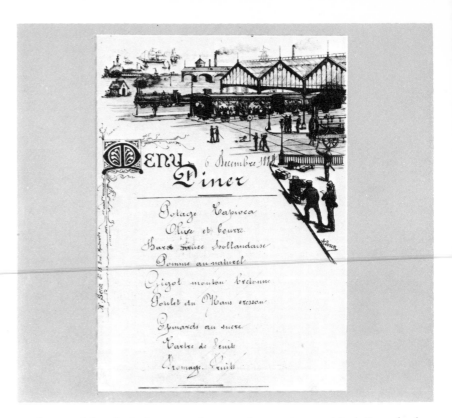

motives, while their immensely popular series entitled Speed also included several cards with a railway theme.

Although cigarette cards were issued by several European countries, few of these ever depicted trains. German cards of the interwar years were largely obsessed with political propaganda, but one of the non-political sets was a mammoth series of 300 cards depicting Railway Wonders of the World, issued by the Garbaty company. Special albums with matching text were provided for these cards and they are now worth a premium. Railways have been depicted on trade cards issued in connection with other kinds of consumer goods from bubble-gum to breakfast cereals, and several of these in recent years have depicted railways.

Railway catering, both in dining-cars, restaurants and hotels, provides many items of ephemera. Most highly prized are the ornate menus used in Pullman's Palace cars of the late nineteenth century and the great European expresses. Though these large-sized menus, sometimes running to several pages, died out during World War I, the later and more functional menu cards should not be despised, giving as they do an interesting picture of the kinds of food and drink (not to mention the prices) associated with railway catering over the years. Paper napkins, coasters and beer mats decorated with company insignia are becoming very elusive and they are doubly desirable when they bear inscriptions and motifs commemorating outstanding contemporary events, such as railway centenaries and the Olympic or Commonwealth Games.

Railway packaging includes special wrappers for newspapers and other urgent freight. Apart from the parcel stamps mentioned in Chapter 6, there are countless different parcel and luggage labels, affixed in order to ensure that these items arrived at the correct destination. Many of the old British companies had specially printed labels for each station, and the more important stations also had sets of labels inscribed to every other conceivable terminus, the labels being printed on paper of different colours coded according to the company whose line was used. Many of the world's railways had colourful transit labels, labels used on luggage carried by both train and steamship, as well as distinctive labels used at company hotels.

Though British railways used a system of tickets to reserve seats for passengers, other countries have had thin card labels which are inserted in special slots on the overhead luggage rack. These seat reservation labels may also be found with a wide variety of destinations inscribed on them. In a similar category come the large cards tacked to wagons and goods trucks to indicate their destination, their cargo or their disposal. Green cards, for example, were widely used in Britain to denote wagons requiring to be sent to the workshops for repair.

Commemorative cards and menus were produced to celebrate the landmarks in a railway's development, particularly the opening or extension of a line or an important anniversary. A few rare cards, however, were produced for events of a very different kind. These include the *in memoriam* cards edged in black with intricate embossed and cut-paper work, produced in memory of the victims of some of the early rail disasters. Cards of this type were fashionable in the nineteenth century as funeral notices.

The most important group of ephemera consists of the prospectuses, annual reports and statements to shareholders, many of which were beautifully printed in order to bolster public confidence. Similarly, railway stock and share certificates rank among the great masterpieces of security printing and the engraver's art. At the height of the railway mania that swept Europe and America in the mid-nineteenth century hundreds of companies were formed and then disappeared spectacularly, leaving duped investors with nothing but handfuls of handsome share certificates as mementoes. Though worthless at the time, these beautiful documents now change hands for real money – often far exceeding the amount for which they were originally issued.

Above Black-edged and embossed memorial card listing the victims of the crash at Clayton Tunnel on the London and Brighton Railway, 25 August 1861

Below Debenture certificate for £500 issued by the Stockton and Hartlepool Railway, October 1839

The QUEBEC BRIDGE

Spanning the
ST. LAWRENCE RIVER

9 Railway souvenirs

Although stamps, medals and printed ephemera provide many examples of rail memento, there are numerous three-dimensional souvenirs ranging from fine art to downright kitsch but all are relevant to a collection of railway antiques. It is difficult at this distance in time to appreciate the tremendous impact of the railways in the mid-nineteenth century. They epitomized the Industrial Revolution more than any other single innovation and captured the imagination of artists and craftsmen in many media.

The railways and various facets of rail travel were a fertile source of inspiration to the genre and narrative painters of the Victorian era. Landscape paintings dominated by locomotives with smoke billowing from their tall stacks vied with stage-coaches as a popular subject in the 1850s. Many artists concentrated on the interiors of railway carriages. Narrative paintings, such as *The Travelling Companions* by Augustus Egg or *To Brighton and Back for 3/6* by Charles Rossiter capture the flavour of early rail travel in first- and third-class coaches respectively.

If original oil paintings with a railway theme are now on the expensive side, there are many water-colours and gouaches available for relatively modest sums. The most desirable are those which formed the basis of well-known railway posters and they are still being produced to this day, though they reached their peak in the 1930s.

The railways were a popular subject of aquatints, mezzotints and chromolithographs. Early editions of railway prints by Currier and Ives are the most highly prized in this class, but there are many other engravings and lithographs by lesser publishers which are worth looking for. Many of the railway companies themselves published such prints, either suitably mounted for framing or reproduced as part of their annual calendars. The calendars themselves are of great interest since they often bore advertising matter below the picture and on the back. At the lower end of the scale there are the old-style company Christmas and other greetings cards which frequently reproduced paintings of railway scenes.

The dramatic rise of the railways in nineteenth-century England coincided with the growth of the ceramics industry. The potteries of the industrial belt in the North Midlands, where the development

Above Calendar published by the Rock Island Line for 1888

Opposite Pamphlet commemorating the Quebec Bridge over the St Lawrence River, published by the Canadian National Railways, 1898

Mug depicting *William IV*, an engine by Braithwaite and Ericson, which was ordered for the Manchester and Liverpool line but was delivered too late for the opening ceremony in 1829

of the railways was at its height, were not slow in depicting this new medium of transport on their tableware and hollow-ware. Early railways, bridges and the façades of stations were a popular form of decoration on mugs, jugs, tankards, shaving mugs and dishes, rackplates, vases and bowls. The majority were probably produced to popularize the subject and had a general pictorial concept, but the most desirable items were produced in connection with a specific occasion such as the opening of a line, the formation of a company, the inauguration of a viaduct or the establishment of a station. The pottery of the late nineteenth century was more sophisticated and tended to commemorate jubilees and other important anniversaries such as the birth centenary of George Stephenson and other railway pioneers. Tin-glazed earthenware and transfer-printed creamware were followed by ornate porcelain plates. This custom was by no means confined to Britain. Relatively little railway pottery seems to have emanated from Europe, but it was a popular subject in North America, and it is significant that the largest sale of railway pottery in recent years took place in Toronto in 1967. In the twentieth century there was a shift of emphasis away from the potteries to the railway companies themselves, and from the late 1920s onwards many of them, especially in America, celebrated their centenaries with commemorative plates. One should not overlook commemorative pottery of a more general nature which incorporated a railway theme. Thus the Tyneside potteries produced plates publicizing the Newcastle Exhibition of 1929, showing the famous railway bridge over the Tyne and featuring a modern locomotive as one of the vignettes round the edge. The revival of interest in commemorative pottery in recent years has induced the pottery and porcelain manufacturers to issue limited editions of plates, and the 150th anniversary of the Stockton and Darlington Railway was celebrated in this way in the year 1975.

Curiously enough very few potlids of the nineteenth century had a railway theme, an exception being the lid in the London series depicting Charing Cross station. A few china fairings incorporate early locomotives and railway carriages.

Railway bridges and viaducts, rather than the trains and locomotives themselves, were the subject of enamelled and engraved glassware of the mid-nineteenth century, a variation on the theme of the Sunderland Bridge which had been a popular subject in this medium from the 1790s onwards. The invention of moulded and pressed glass techniques in America, however, gave rise to bottles, flasks, custard dishes and paperweights featuring locomotives. There were even hollow glass jars in the shape of a locomotive and these were used as candy containers. The lid was sometimes made of tinware, enamelled with a view of the interior of the cab. Many of the paperweights consisted of simple shallow domes or slabs of bevelled glass with a chromolithograph of a railway scene fixed to the base. At

the turn of the century tinted sepia photographs were often used instead but these are not so desirable.

Not all paperweights were made of glass, and there are many examples to be found in cast iron, bronze or brass, either depicting a locomotive or a three-dimensional representation of an animal or some other motif which was the emblem of a railway company. Many of these metal paperweights were produced by the companies as advertising gimmicks in the early years of this century. Other forms of metalwork, inspired by the railways but seldom produced directly by them, include massive cast-iron doorstops and door porters of the mid-nineteenth century. Door knockers showing an early locomotive were produced in iron, brass and bronze. Engines and carriages were featured on horse brasses, and many different varieties of these talismans have been produced from the late nineteenth century down to the present day.

Inevitably, any decorative surface on objects of the mid-nineteenth century may be found with a railway theme. Trains were a popular subject for the pictorial fan-leaves in the 1830s and 40s, and similar scenes may be found on bandboxes, hatboxes and glove boxes of the same vintage or even later. Union cases of *bois durci* and other proto-plastics often depicted locomotives in the 1850s and 60s. Cigar boxes, cheroot cases, snuffboxes and cigarette cases made of silver had inlaid or chased decoration showing early trains; others had *repoussé* ornament with the same theme or were delicately carved in ivory in low relief. Locomotives were also embossed in gold leaf on leather or inlaid or enamelled on metal plaques for cigar cases and card cases. Apart from the matchbox labels and matchbooks which are discussed in the previous chapter there are several distinct types of metal matchbox. Early examples in silver, brass or white metal had railway scenes engraved on their sides, and a few novelty

Part of a shaving set depicting Stephenson's *Rocket* and the passenger carriages; (centre) a mug showing the *Northumbrian* which George Stephenson drove at the opening ceremony of the London and Manchester Railway, 5 September 1830.

Above Printed cotton handkerchief showing a map of the railways in Britain; undated, but *c.* 1846 judging by the routes depicted

matchboxes of the late nineteenth century were actually fashioned in the shape of locomotives. Other novelty matchboxes were of copper sheet enamelled with a design simulating railway tickets. Many of the railway companies in an era before the matchbook issued tin matchboxes with transfer-printed motifs bearing the company insignia.

The most expensive rarities are the large trophies and presentation pieces in silver or silver-gilt which formerly graced many a directors' boardroom. Some of them were exact scale models of locomotives, correct to the smallest detail; others were replicas of railway stations or bridges. More plentiful, however, are the silver salvers, cake baskets, cups and tankards whose inscriptions record long and faithful service to the railway company. Cigarette boxes may be found modelled as silver tenders or goods wagons, and there are even musical boxes disguised as freight trucks, railcars and locomotives. The Kremlin Armoury Museum, Moscow, displays a Fabergé Easter egg made for Tsar Nicholas II in 1900. It opens to reveal a gold and platinum replica of the Trans-Siberian Railway train, exquisitely jeweled and enamelled, its clockwork motor, with the precision of a Swiss watch, operated by a golden key.

At first glance furniture seems a most unlikely souvenir of the railways, but apart from the chairs and footstools bearing company crests and inscriptions used on the trains there are comparatively rare nineteenth-century chairs whose backs are painted or inlaid in marquetry with vintage locomotives. This was a popular feature of rockers in mid-nineteenth-century New England, but other items which have been noted with a railway theme include firescreens, work-boxes and writing-cases in wood or papier mâché with painted or inlaid motifs.

Textiles also yield their quota of railway collectables. Snuff kerchiefs and handkerchiefs in printed silks and cottons were popular at the time the railways made their début, so it was fitting that locomotives, bridges and route maps should become popular subjects – varying considerably in their accuracy. In more recent times railways have been featured on table-cloths, tea-towels and even

Right Souvenir rulers in metal and ivorine, published by the Minneapolis and St Louis, the Rock Island Line and the Gulf, Mobile and Ohio Railroads

polishing cloths. At the present time they are among the more popular souvenirs of the narrow-gauge light railways, the preservation societies and the railway museums.

Stevengraphs, the woven silk pictures of Thomas Stevens and other manufacturers such as W. H. Grant, depicted many railway subjects including named locomotives like Stephenson's *Rocket* and *Locomotion No. 1*. One of these Stevengraphs, captioned 'Stephenson's Triumph', depicted the *Lord Howe* locomotive and was produced for the York Exhibition of 1879. Almost a century later Stevengraphs have been revived, and the National Railway Museum publishes a modern version of the *Lord Howe* silk, identical to the original in all but the inscription.

Crested spoons, enamelled badges, cloth patches, rulers, pens and pencils are among the minor souvenirs either produced by the railway companies as giveaways or by the manufacturers of fancy goods cashing in on a perennially favourite topic. They vary enormously both in quality and tastefulness, and those that actually advertise a specific company are decidedly preferable; but any novelty – from erasers and pencil sharpeners to salts and peppers – with a railway motif is of interest, real or potential. For the collector whose space is really limited an interesting array of miniature locomotives in gold and silver for charm bracelets and other forms of jewelry could be formed but not without considerable patience, ingenuity and cost.

Above Liverpool porcelain milk jug, depicting the Manchester and Liverpool Railway

Left Double Stevengraph woven at the York Exhibition, 1879, commemorating the London–York mail coach of 1706 and the Stockton–Darlington train of 1825

Tin-plate toy train *Victoria*, manufactured by Bing of Germany, *c.* 1890

10 Railway models

Within a few years of their invention locomotives were beginning to appear in model and toy form. The earliest were pull-along toy trains carved from solid blocks of wood and stained or varnished without any other decoration. Wooden trains of this basic type have continued up to the present time, but the plain, dark wood was soon transformed by painting in bright colours or the use of transfers. Few of the early wooden toy trains have survived in pristine condition, but it is better to leave the original paintwork, even though badly flaked, than attempt to replace it.

Clockwork models in enamelled or transfer-printed tin-plate first appeared in England about 1840, though they were actually manufactured in Germany. They operated without rails and moved in a circle, tied to a central point. Small brass locomotives were also produced commercially in Britain about the same time and these were actually powered by steam. The earliest models had no rails and were designed to run on the floor, being fitted with serrated wheels which gave a better grip. They were equipped with bulbous pot boilers externally fired by small spirit lamps and were nicknamed Birmingham Dribblers after the city of their origin and their bad habit of leaking. They were usually made from brass castings with the lower part of the boiler alone soldered to the chassis. One had to be very careful to check that the boiler never ran dry, or else the heat would melt the solder, and the boiler would disintegrate. The earliest examples had two small and two large wheels, oscillating cylinders and hand-rolled or soldered tubes with a side seam. After 1850 machine-made drawn tubes without seams came into use. After 1870 they were almost entirely machine-made and became more complex with additional wheels, water tanks, fixed cylinders and proper valves (either eccentric valve gear or Stephenson's link motion).

At the turn of the century these miniature steam-engines became increasingly sophisticated and for the first time were modelled fairly closely on real locomotives. From 1895 onwards hand-painting was made easier and more realistic by the provision of small transfers reproducing actual railway insignia. By 1900 it was possible to buy these locomotives in kit form. American models made of cast iron were produced as a sideline by the iron and steel foundries of Connecticut as early as the mid-1840s, and mass production was

German clockwork train set, *c.* 1840

adopted by 1870. These American models were relatively crude in appearance and were of the simple pull-along variety. Most steam-engines were imported from France and Germany where several large firms specialized in their manufacture from about 1890 onwards. They were technically superior to the old Birmingham Dribblers and brought an element of precision engineering into the hobby. By 1910 the steam locomotive had reached the peak of its development but had priced itself out of the mass market.

Its place was taken by greatly improved clockwork trains which from 1880 onward were produced in sets, complete with cars, wagons, coaches, tenders and rails of various gauges. They were made of tin-plate and originated in Germany where Bing and Märklin soon dominated the world market. The earliest tracks had a rather large gauge, but this was reduced and standarized about 1900 when the O gauge was introduced. This gauge soon spread to other countries and led to vast improvements both in the type of track and the variety of rolling-stock. Complicated layouts really date from this period. The earlier 1 and 2 gauges (measuring $1\frac{3}{4}$ in and 2 in respectively) did not die out completely, though they are scarce and now highly prized. Great improvements in clockwork trains were effected by the British companies, such as Lines Brothers, Hornby and Bassett-Lowke, in the early years of this century, and the use of castings instead of the clumsy tin-plate lent greater realism to locomotives and rolling-stock. The much smaller 00 or 'Doublo' gauge was pioneered by the Trix Company in the 1930s and soon followed by other companies. This permitted a greater variety of track layout in a relatively limited space. Electric motors were introduced about 1910 but did not become widespread until after World War I. Pre-1914 examples are now exceedingly rare, but electric train sets of the 1930s are still reasonably plentiful, though

Cast-iron toy train, produced as a side-line of a Connecticut iron foundry, c. 1850

Hornby clockwork locomotive in South-Western Railway livery, and accessories, including footbridge, signals and signal-box, *c.* 1925

worth a premium if still with the original boxes. As electric sets became more sophisticated, there was a further revival of simple clockwork trains immediately before World War II, and many types continue to this day, serving the needs of the youngest children. As such they have attracted little attention from collectors, though examples made of bakelite and urea plastics of the late 1940s and 50s are now worth consideration on technical grounds alone.

The fashion for scale models developed in the early 1900s and divided into two main categories. The ultimate in model engineering was the garden layout, using a fairly large gauge of track and locomotives up to 6 ft or 8 ft in length powered by coal. In the earlier coal-fired locomotives running efficiency was sacrificed for accuracy of scale, but in the 20s this trend was reversed and the size of boiler, grate and working parts became exaggerated in relation to the overall scale in order to improve the running qualities. The largest of these models were used to operate miniature railways capable of carrying real passengers. Some of these are run by private enthusiasts, though many others today form important tourist attractions in various parts of the world.

Left A fine model of the locomotive *Pocasset* of the Northern Railroad; American, *c.* 1890

Below 3½″ gauge model of a coal-fired Great Northern Railway Ivatt Atlantic locomotive

Right Lead alloy figures of a station staff and accessories for a model railway layout, manufactured for the Hornby series by Meccano Limited of Liverpool, *c.* 1936

Below Working model of the Great Northern locomotive *Scorpion*

The other category of models was concerned more with accuracy of detail and less with running efficiency. These models tend to be much smaller and are usually powered by spirit stoves, though coal-firing is by no means unknown. These extremely detailed scale models, often hand-built by experts over a period of years, comprise the most expensive of all railway collectables, and a small fortune can be spent on a complete garden layout together with coaches, rolling-stock and other equipment.

The railway companies commissioned the production of scale models for a number of reasons. The most interesting are the prototypes from which full-sized locomotives might subsequently be developed. Apart from these engineering models there were the display models intended for the company's offices and showrooms, which might be superficially accurate but lacked the intricate machinery of working models.

Associated with scale models and toy trains are the wagons, trucks, carriages, dining-cars, sleeping-cars and brake-vans, the better examples being a tribute to the coachbuilder's art, complete in every detail down to the glass windows and the upholstery. Commercial rolling-stock for toy trains varied enormously in quality and degree of realism, but even the naïve transfer-printed toys of yesteryear have a great deal of charm. The real enthusiast, of course, would always prefer to construct his own stations, depots, signal-boxes, water-towers and signalling equipment, but the toy manufacturers catered to the unskilled by producing these ancillary items in great profusion. These and the tiny lead figures, scaled to the o or oo gauges, reflect in miniature the atmosphere of the real, life-sized railways and as such are an aspect of railway antiques that deserves more serious consideration.

WORCESTER SALT SPECIAL.
162 Cars started by President-Elect, William McKinley.
TRAIN NEARLY ONE AND A HALF MILES LONG.
OVER 5,000,000 lbs WORCESTER SALT PACKED IN 725,613 BAGS, 50,000 CARTONS, 7,000 LARGE SACKS
ENOUGH TO SEASON 100,000,000 lbs. OF BUTTER.
THE BARRELS PILED END ON END   THE BAGS LAID IN A ROW
WOULD BE OVER SIX MILES HIGH.   WOULD EXTEND 131 MILES.
THE LARGEST SINGLE SHIPMENT OF A MANUFACTURED COMMODITY EVER MADE.

TRAIN SHIPPED FROM,
WORCESTER SALT FACTORY, SILVER SPRINGS, N.Y.
JAN. 6TH 1897 VIA ERIE. AND N.Y. N.H. & H.R.R.
TO NEW ENGLAND POINTS.

Museums and societies

There are many clubs and societies in Britain and North America devoted to general and specific aspects of the railways. In the United States, for example, the leading organization is the National Railway Historical Society with its permanent headquarters in Philadelphia, Pa. 19103 (Box 2051). The Society is composed of more than 100 Chapters, ranging from one each in Alaska and Wisconsin to sixteen in Pennsylvania alone. The Society also has a Canadian Chapter based in Laurentide, Quebec province. The nearest British equivalent is the Railway Club at 112 High Holborn, London, WC1. With the exception of the Newcomen Society at the Science Museum, London, SW7, and the Railway and Locomotive Historical Society, Harvard University, Cambridge, Massachusetts, the other clubs do not have a permanent address. They hold meetings and exhibitions in various parts of the country. Details of their activities and the names and addresses of their current secretaries can be obtained from one or other of the railway periodicals listed in the Reading list.

The British societies dealing with specialized and general aspects of the railways include the following:

Historical Model Railway Society
Locomotive Club of Great Britain
Model Railway Club
Railway and Canal Historical Society
Railway Correspondence and Travel Society
Railway Philatelic Group
Railway Society of Scotland
Signalling Record Society
Stephenson Locomotive Society
Transport Ticket Society

In addition to regular programmes of meetings and outings to sites of railway interest these clubs and societies publish their own bulletins, journals and newsletters and have even undertaken the publication of catalogues and monographs of immense value to the collector and railway student.

The number of preservation societies continues to grow steadily from year to year, and the mileage of track operated is growing at a corresponding rate. A significant factor is the number of these light

Opposite Framed poster of January 1897 advertising the American Worcester Salt Special – a train nearly 1½ miles long carrying 5,000,000 lb of salt – a world record shipment of a manufactured commodity at that time

railways which have 'gone public' in recent years, becoming serious commercial undertakings which offer a very real service to the public. Many of the preservation societies operating these lines have restored old depots and stations as museums. The lines themselves may be regarded as working museums with historic locomotives and rolling-stock which have been lovingly restored to full running order. The preserved lines of Britain include the following:

Bluebell Railway (Sussex)
Dart Valley Railway (Devon)
Festiniog Railway (North Wales)
Keighley and Worth Valley Light Railway (Yorkshire)
Lochty Railway (Fife, Scotland)
Middleton Railway Trust (Lancashire)
Romney, Hythe and Dymchurch (Kent)
Severn Valley Railway (Shropshire, West Midlands)
Snowdon Mountain Railway (North Wales)
Strathspey Railway (Inverness-shire)
Talyllyn Railway (North Wales)
Vale of Rheidol (North Wales)
Welshpool and Llanfair Railway (Montgomeryshire)
West Somerset Railway (Somerset)

There are about a dozen museums in Britain and a score in North America which are devoted specifically to railway relics, many of them in converted loco sheds and depots. In the list which follows those which operate working locomotives and rolling-stock, giving rides to visitors on authentic trains of bygone days, are marked with an asterisk.

Britain
* Beamish Museum, Chester-le-Street, Co. Durham
* Bressingham Hall, Diss, Norfolk
Great Western Railway Museum, Swindon
* Locomotive Museum, Penrhyn Castle
Museum of Science and Industry, Birmingham
Museum of Technology for the East Midlands, Leicester
Museum of Transport, Glasgow
National Railway Museum, York
Pendon Museum, Abingdon, Berkshire
Science and Engineering Museum, Newcastle upon Tyne
Science Museum, South Kensington, London
Steamtown, Carnforth, Lancashire
* Tramways Museum, Crich, Derbyshire

Canada
* Canadian Railway Museum, St Constant, Quebec

United States of America
Baltimore and Ohio Transportation Museum, Baltimore, Maryland
* Boothbay Railway Museum, Boothbay, Maine
* California Railway Museum, Rio Vista, Berkeley, California
Casey Jones Home Railroad Museum, Jackson, Tennessee
Colorado Railroad Museum, Golden, Colorado
Conneaut Railroad Museum, Conneaut, Ohio
* Edaville Railroad Museum, South Carver, Massachusetts
* Illinois Railway Museum, Union, Illinois
* Indiana Railway Museum, Greensburg, Indiana
Lake Shore Railway Historical Society, North East, Pennsylvania
Lake Superior Museum of Transportation and Industry, Duluth,
    Minnesota
* Mid-Continent Railway Museum, North Freedom, Wisconsin
National Railroad Museum, Green Bay, Wisconsin
* Ohio Railway Museum, Worthington, Ohio
Pate Museum of Transportation, Fort Worth, Texas
* Puget Sound and Snoqualmie Valley Railroad, Snoqualmie,
    Seattle, Washington
* Railways to Yesterday, Orbisonia, Allentown, Pennsylvania
Roanoke Transportation Museum, Wasena Park, Roanoke, Virginia
* Tennessee Valley Railroad Museum, Chattanooga, Tennessee

Australia
Railways Historical Museum, Adelaide, South Australia
Railway Museum, Enfield, New South Wales

New Zealand
* Kingston Flyer (steam train operated in the summer months
    between Kingston and Lumsden)
* Tramways Museum, Paekakariki

South Africa
Jimmie Hall Museum of Transport, Johannesburg

Reading list

From the prospectuses and reports of the 1820s to the picture books of today the railways have inspired a vast amount of literature, from general works to detailed histories of individual lines. Space prevents the listing of more than a mere fraction of that output, and the books given below are those in the English language which give rather more prominence to the collectable aspects of the railways. Several publishers have specialized in railway books, notably Howell-North Books of Berkeley, California and David and Charles of Newton Abbott, Devon and Ian Allan of Shepperton, Surrey. Detailed railway bibliographies include the excellent catalogue by George Ottley, published by Allen & Unwin in 1965. The Association of American Railroads, Washington, D.C., produces a railway bibliography which is free on request.

Alexander, Edwin P. *The Collector's Book of the Locomotive*, Clarkson Potter, New York, 1966

Baker, Stanley L. and Kunz, Virginia B. *The Collector's Book of Railroadiana*, Hawthorn Books, New York, 1976

Beebe, Lucius *Mr. Pullman's Elegant Palace Car*, Doubleday, New York, 1961
Mansions on Rails, Howell-North, Berkeley, 1959
Highball: A Pageant of Trains, Crown, New York, 1945

Berghaus, Erwin *The History of Railways*, Barrie & Rockliff, London, 1964

Dean, S. C. and Gard, R. M. *The Stockton and Darlington Railway*, Newcastle University, 1975

Dubin, Arthur D. *Some Classic Trains*, Kalmbach, Milwaukee, 1964
More Classical Trains, Kalmbach, Milwaukee, 1974

Haresnape, Brian *Railway Design since 1830*, Ian Allan, Shepperton, 1969 (2 vols)

Harlow, Alvin F. *Old Waybills*, Appleton-Century, New York, 1934

Hertz, Louis H. *Collecting Model Trains*, Simmons-Boardman, New York, 1956

Hornung, Clarence P. *Wheels across America*, Barnes, New York, 1959

Kinert, Reed *Early American Steam Locomotives*, Crown, New York, 1962

O'Connell, John *Railroad Album*, Popular Mechanics, Chicago, 1954

Page, Martin *The Lost Pleasures of the Great Trains*, Weidenfeld & Nicolson, London, 1976

Shaw, Frederic *Casey Jones' Locker*, Hesperian, San Francisco, 1959

Smith, Donald J. *Discovering Railwayana*, Shire, Tring, 1971

Whitehouse, P. B. (ed.) *Railway Relics and Regalia (Country Life)*, London, 1975

Williams, Peter *Britain's Railway Museums*, Ian Allan, Shepperton, 1975

Ziel, Ron *The Twilight of the Steam Locomotive*, Grossett & Dunlap, New York, 1963

American periodicals

Great World of Model Railroading
Model Railroad Craftsman
Model Railroader
Passenger Train Journal
Rail Classics
Rail Fan
Railroad Magazine
Railroad Modeler
Trains

British periodicals

Model Railway Constructor
Model Railways
Modern Railways
Modern Tramways and Light Railways Review
Railway Gazette
Railway Magazine
Railway Modeller
Railway World
Trains Illustrated

Acknowledgments

The author and publisher would like to thank the following museums, collections and photographers by whose courtesy the illustrations in the book are reproduced:

American Museum in Britain, 6, 37 *left*, 89, **104**, 126

Author's Collection, 11 *bottom*, 22, 74, 76 *left*, 77 *both*, 79, 81, 82, 83, **85**, 88 *both*, 90, 91 *bottom*, 92, 93, 95 *both*, 96, 97 *both*, 98 *both*, 100, 101 *top*, 106 *both*, 107 *right*, 108 *bottom*, 109 *jacket (top right)*

Stanley L. Baker Collection, 28, 58, 61 *top*, 66 *left*, 69 *bottom*, 71, 72 *top*, 73, 84 *top right*, 88 *top*, 87, 89 *top*, 91 *top*, **104**, 113, 116 *bottom*

Commemorative Pottery 1780–1900, John and Jennifer May (Heinemann, 1972), 114, 115 *centre right*

Compagnie Internationale des Wagons-Lits et du Tourisme, 42, 107 *bottom*, 110

George Dow Collection, *jacket (top left)*

Glasgow Museums and Art Galleries, 47, 60

Geoffrey Godden, 26, 117 *both*

Museum of Childhood, Menai Bridge, 118

Ironbridge Gorge Museum Trust, **86**

Lincoln Train Museum, Gettysburg, Pennsylvania, 122–3 *top*

Mansell Collection, 18, 21, 115 *top left*, *endpapers*, *jacket flap*

Merseyside County Museums, 115 *centre right*

Milton Bradley Company, 27

National Railway Museum, York (Crown Copyright), 1, 2, 4, 23, 25, 29, 32 *both*, 33, 34, 35, 36, 37 *right*, 38 *top*, 39 *both*, 41, 43, 45, 48, 50, 51 *both*, 52, 53 *top*, 54, 55, 59, 61 *bottom*, 62 *both*, 63, 64, 65, 66 *top*, 67, 68, 69 *top*, 72 *bottom*, 76 *top*, 80, 84 *left*, 90 *right*, 101 *bottom*, 111 *both*, 116 *top*, *jacket (centre, bottom left and right)*

Phillips Auctioneers, London, 124–5 *bottom*

Public Archives of Canada, 105, 108 *top*, 112

Shelburne Museum Inc., Shelburne, Vermont, 120–1 *bottom*

Robert A. Smith, 13

Sotheby & Co., 115 *top right and bottom*

Sotheby's Belgravia, 30, 38 *bottom*, 57, 107 *top left*, 121 *top*, 122–3 *bottom*, 124 *top*, 136

D. Thompson, 11 *centre*, 15, 16–17, 134–5

Union Pacific Railroad Museum Collection, 11 *top*, 49, 53 *bottom*, **103**, *jacket (back)*

United States Signal Corps Photo (Brady Collection), 8–9

Victoria and Albert Museum (Crown Copyright), 119

References to colour plates are in **bold type**.

Index

Page numbers in italic refer to illustrations.

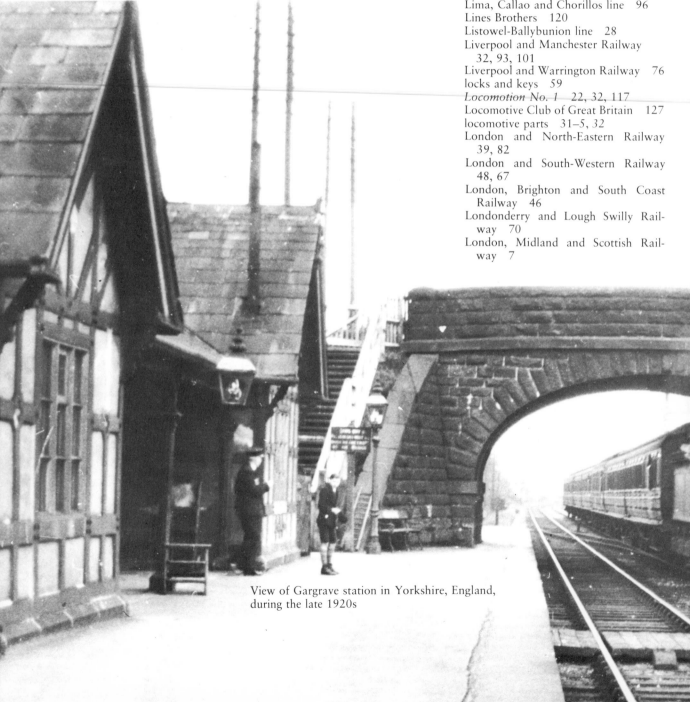

View of Gargrave station in Yorkshire, England, during the late 1920s

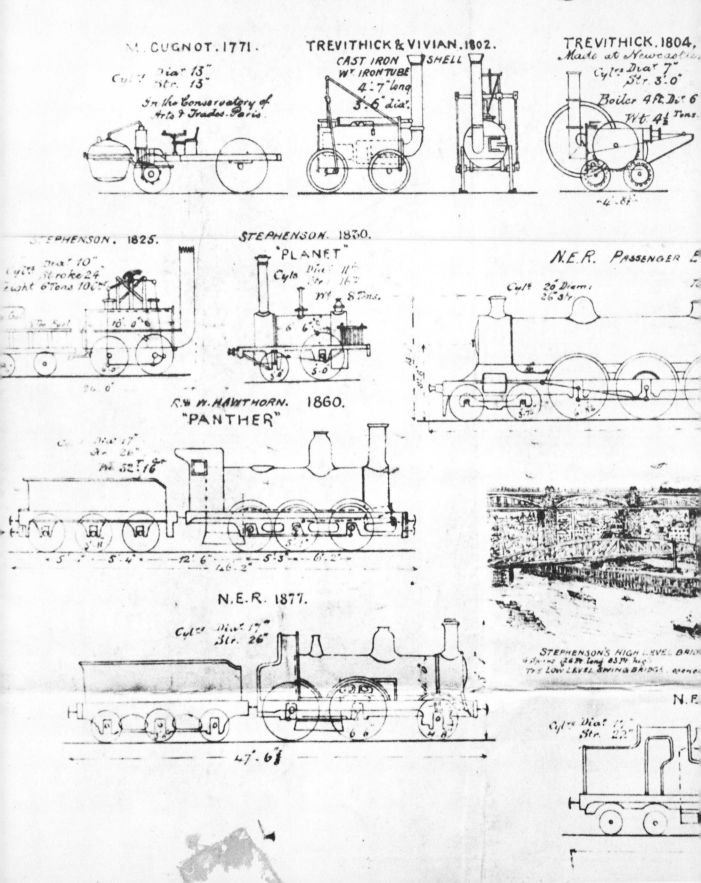

M. CUGNOT. 1771.

Cyl᷑ Dia᷑ 13"
Cyl᷑ Str. 13"

In the Conservatory of
Arts & Trades. Paris.

TREVITHICK & VIVIAN. 1802.

CAST IRON SHELL
W᷑ IRON TUBE
4': 7" long
3': 6" dia᷑

TREVITHICK. 1804,

Made at Newcastle
Cyl᷑s Dia᷑ 7"
Str. 3.0"
Boiler 4 Ft. Di᷑ 6
Wt. 4½ Tons.

~4'. 8½"

STEPHENSON. 1825.

Cyl᷑s Dia᷑ 10"
Stroke 24
Weight 6 Tons 10C᷑

10'. 0"

24. 0"

STEPHENSON. 1830.
"PLANET"

Cyls Dia᷑ 11"
Str. 16½"
Wt. 8 Tons.

6'. 6"

5'. 0"

N.E.R. PASSENGER E

Cyl᷑ 26 Diam:
26 Str.

R. & W. HAWTHORN. 1860.
"PANTHER"

Cyl᷑s Dia᷑ 17"
Str. 26"
Wt. 32 T. 16

5'
5'. 4"
12'. 6"
5'. 3"
6'. 2"
46. 2"

N.E.R. 1877.

Cyl᷑s Dia᷑ 17"
Str. 26"

47'. 6⅛"

STEPHENSON'S HIGH LEVEL BRIDGE
6 Spans 126 Ft. long 85 Ft. high
THE LOW LEVEL SWING BRIDGE, opened

N.E.

Cyl᷑ Dia᷑ 17"
Str. 22"